THE NORMAN WAIT HARRIS
MEMORIAL FOUNDATION

THE Harris Foundation Lectures at the University of Chicago have been made possible through the generosity of the heirs of Norman Wait Harris and Emma Gale Harris, who donated to the University a fund to be known as "The Norman Wait Harris Memorial Foundation" on January 27, 1923. The letter of gift contains the following statement:

It is apparent that a knowledge of world-affairs was never of more importance to Americans than today. The spirit of distrust which pervades the Old World is not without its effect upon our own country. How to combat this disintegrating tendency is a problem worthy of the most serious thought. Perhaps one of the best methods is the promotion of a better understanding of other nations through wisely directed educational effort.

The purpose of the foundation shall be the promotion of a better understanding on the part of American citizens of the other peoples of the world, thus establishing a basis for improved international relations and a more enlightened world-order. The aim shall always be to give accurate information, not to propagate opinion.

Annual Institutes have been held at the University of Chicago since the summer of 1924. This series of volumes includes the lectures there delivered, in essentially their original form.

POPULATION

THE UNIVERSITY OF CHICAGO PRESS
CHICAGO, ILLINOIS

—

THE BAKER & TAYLOR COMPANY
NEW YORK

THE CAMBRIDGE UNIVERSITY PRESS
LONDON

THE MARUZEN-KABUSHIKI-KAISHA
TOKYO, OSAKA, KYOTO, FUKUOKA, SENDAI

THE COMMERCIAL PRESS, LIMITED
SHANGHAI

POPULATION

[LECTURES ON THE HARRIS FOUNDATION 1929]

By

CORRADO GINI, *President of the Central Statistical Bureau, Rome, Italy;* SHIROSHI NASU, *Professor of Rural Economics, Imperial University of Tokyo, Japan;* ROBERT R. KUCZYNSKI, *Council Member, Institute of Economics, Washington, D.C.;* OLIVER E. BAKER, *Economic Geographer, Bureau of Agricultural Economics, Department of Agriculture, Washington, D.C.*

THE UNIVERSITY OF CHICAGO PRESS
CHICAGO · ILLINOIS

COMPOSED AND PRINTED BY THE UNIVERSITY OF CHICAGO PRESS
CHICAGO, ILLINOIS, U.S.A.

FOREWORD

The first four institutes on the Harris Foundation dealt respectively with European, Far Eastern, Mexican, and British Empire affairs. The fifth institute, in 1928, instead of limiting itself to a particular region or state, dealt with a general topic, "Foreign Investments"; and the sixth institute, from June 17 to June 28, 1929, was similarly organized. The topic chosen on the latter occasion was "Population Problems"; and the lectures, reproduced in this volume, discuss the theory of population growth and decline on the basis of statistical, social, and biological data. Certain practical problems involved in the relation of population to agriculture and resources, and in their mutual adjustment, are also dealt with.

The qualifications of the authors to speak authoritatively on the subjects with which they deal are in part indicated on the title-page. Professor Gini has come to be recognized on the continent of Europe and throughout the world as a leading statistician. He has written numerous articles on statistical and population problems and is editor-in-chief of *Metron*. His works on *The Demographic Factors in the Evolution of the Nations* (1911) and

FOREWORD

on *The Amount and Composition of the Wealth of the Nations* (1914) were awarded the Royal Prize of the Academy of the Lincei for Social Sciences (1919), which is the highest award for scientific works in Italy. He is professor of statistics at the University of Rome and, as president of the Central Statistical Bureau of Rome, is in close relations with the chief of the Italian government. Professor Nasu is a recognized authority on agricultural and population problems in Japan, on which he has written extensively. Dr. Kuczynski was formerly director of the Municipal Statistical Office at Berlin-Schoenberg. His work in the statistical analysis of population movements extends over many years, and his recently published *The Balance of Births and Deaths* has emphasized the significance of some hitherto neglected factors in forecasting the growth of populations. He has also contributed in the field of financial statistics and was among the Harris Foundation lecturers at the fifth institute, in 1928. Dr. Baker, an expert on agricultural areas and agricultural production in the United States, has made important comparative studies of land utilization in different countries.

QUINCY WRIGHT, *Executive Secretary*

TABLE OF CONTENTS

THE CYCLICAL RISE AND FALL
OF POPULATION

By CORRADO GINI

INTRODUCTION

The future of the white race arouses anxiety among students of vital statistics and the ever growing public interested in population problems, caused by two diametrically opposite opinions. Some see the future overshadowed by the threatening danger of overpopulation. They anxiously estimate the maximum number of inhabitants of the white race who could subsist in the lands inhabited by, or habitable by, them; and they come to the disconsolate conclusion that if a world-wide calamity is to be avoided, it is essential that the exuberant birth-rate be scientifically limited (1). On the other hand are those who not less anxiously foresee that our race will cease to increase, almost immediately in the case of the nations of Western and Northern Europe, and, not improbably, in a more distant future in the case of several other populations; and they carry on an active propaganda and call for energetic government action to stimulate the birth-rate in the hopes of postponing the danger which threatens the white race of being submerged by the colored peoples (2). These two opposite forecasts and programs generally correspond to two different theories of population, though these theories are not necessarily connected with the programs from the standpoint of logic.

The first may be described as the *theory of the geometric increase of population*, inasmuch as it starts from the premise that population always tends to multiply in geometric ratio and, indeed, that, as a matter of fact, all peoples would thus multiply if they were not hindered by adverse conditions. This, it is well known, is one of the foundations on which the Malthusian edifice rests. It has been said that such a law constitutes a "truism." As a matter of fact, it is anything but a truism. On the contrary, it presupposes a hypothesis of the most tremendous import—the hypothesis that the reproductive powers of populations remain constant throughout their generations (3).

The second theory denies this premise and considers that facts prove that the reproductive powers of the populations of the world follow a cyclical movement, more or less analogous to that of individuals. This may be described as the *theory of the cyclical rise and fall of population*.

I have been, and I am, a convinced supporter of the theory of the cyclical rise and fall of population, and for the past twenty years and more I have tried to collect facts and arguments in its support

tion speaks. The Etruscan sages, Plutarch tells us, learned precisely that there are several races of men, the one different from the other, in life and customs, and that God has allotted to each its time, which is limited to the period of the "great year," after which there happens the renovation of the world and the change in the human races (5). Someone went even so far as to think that the extension of such a period cannot only be recognized but can even be measured for the Mediterranean civilizations (to which belong the Egyptian, the Greek, the Roman, and those of modern Europe), for those of the Near East (to which belong the Babylonian and Assyrian, the Persian, the Etruscan, the Jewish, and the Arabian), and also for those of India and of Mexico, with the result that the periods would be of an analogous duration in the various parts of the world and, for these and other reasons, they would appear to be due to human nature more than to the environment (6).

Moreover, recent research seems to show that the same parabola described by a people as a whole is also described by the families who compose it; in their case also, and not only in that of royal families and those belonging to the aristocracy and the upper classes, but also in families belonging to the bourgeoisie and to the peasantry, a phase of vigorous growth is followed by one of more or less rapid exhaustion.

A like parabola is also noted, or at least presumed, in the case of other animal species. The data collected by paleontologists have made one think for a long time past of a similar course in the development of some groups of animals whose fossil remains show them to have been the dominant factors in certain geological epochs, but who in the progress of time decline and frequently disappear, or leave only a few remains of their forms.

For some of these species biologists have also been able to note a decline in variability and adaptability to the environment, which would indeed explain their decline and disappearance.

And especially significant, although in some points their interpretation is not very clear, are the experiments made in laboratories on the populations of certain kinds of flies, yeasts, and bacteria. These are particularly well suited to such observations on account of the rapidity with which they propagate. For the populations of bacteria and yeasts the existence of a maximum density has been ascertained, wherein the reproduction of the individuals would not cease but would be exactly compensated by the deaths which are oc-

curring. The m   um could be surpassed only
in special condi   , and only temporarily, and
to it, as to a co   on of stable equilibrium, the
population woul   d to return. Quite a number
of experiments h   demonstrated that such a limit is due to interr   factors, depending on the living
organisms themselves and not on the surrounding
factors (such as lack of space, scarcity of nourishment, presence of refuse products or corpses), although some of these factors, just as temperature,
may influence the greater or lesser rapidity with
which the maximum is arrived at. When the maximum is attained, the population would show,
sooner or later, a decline, so that one may speak,
even for these populations, of three stages, corresponding to youth, adult age, and senility. The
course of the population during these stages, as
well as the maximum of density that it may attain, would differ for the various species of bacteria, and, in some species, also for various races
(7). The same would happen, for certain species
of flies, for which the curve of development was
even described and studied up to the point of saturation (8).

The slow exhaustion of the reproductive powers
of human populations and of animal species, that
is to say, of their germinal cells, seems, moreover,

very natural when we reflect that these cells have a common origin and probably, at the start, the identical constitution of the somatic cells, so that, if the life of the latter be limited, it would indeed be strange if the former were able to live and multiply indefinitely.

The fact that the germinal cells and the somatic cells are exposed in an essentially different degree to the differentiating action of the environment may explain why the latter have so rapid an evolution, corresponding to the life of the individual, while the evolution of the former embraces such a much longer period as that of the life of the population or species group.

A fact which needs to be explained is why the reproductive powers, which for the somatic cells are steadily declining in the individual life, are, on the contrary, for the germinal cells increasing in the first phase of the development of populations. The explanation is to be found in the consideration that fecundity, like all other characteristics, is to some extent hereditary; but in the case in point, heredity has this special result, that each generation consists in a greater degree than its predecessor of the descendants of prolific individuals, so that the average fecundity of the population becomes higher.

We thus see that, during a first period, the

tendency of fecundity to increase, as a result of the influence of the hereditary factor, is greater than the tendency to decline, which is due to the natural exhaustion of reproductive powers; but, in a subsequent period, the two opposing forces will balance; and, finally, physiological exhaustion will gain the upper hand.

The length of the cycle of evolution of populations compared to the brief period for which statistical data were available at the beginning of last century, and the scanty information then available on primitive populations, even scantier than that we now possess, explain why the evolution of the reproductive tendency escaped the attention of Malthus; the same reasons explain how it is that it still escapes the attention of many students who confine themselves to the white race in modern times.

On another occasion I compared the error they commit to that which a flea, or other animal whose life cycle is very brief compared to that of man, would commit if, watching the growth of a baby, it were to estimate its future size on the hypothesis that its rate of growth would remain constant in the future; then, on the basis of this supposition, it should be concerned with the thought that sooner or later no rooms, or houses, or other buildings could be raised which would be capable of housing that body which was to go on growing indefinitely.

The foregoing considerations will serve as a basis and introduction to the three lectures which I undertook to hold here when I accepted the honor of the invitation so kindly extended to me by the Harris Foundation.

They will deal with the birth, evolution, and death of nations—the word "nations" to be understood as a group of men having a personality not only from a political and cultural but also from a biological aspect. But the advisability of beginning with the best-known phase induces me to depart from that which would be the natural order of these lectures, and to start by dealing with the intermediate phase relating to the evolution of nations.

NOTES

1. The last work of Sir G. H. Knibbs, *The Shadow of the World's Future* (London: E. Benn, 1928), can be considered as one of the best statements of this thesis. The author has confirmed and developed ideas repeatedly explained in preceding articles and in particular in the article, "The Theory of Large Population Aggregates" in *Metron*, 1-VII-1920, Vol. I, N. 1.

2. In Germany and in Italy, especially through the prefaces by O. Spengler and by Mussolini to the German edition and the Italian translation, respectively, the pamphlet by R. Korherr, *Geburtenrückgang* (*Süddeutsche Monatshefte*) (München: Coffmann), has been widely noticed. The Italian translation is entitled: *Regresso delle nascite, Morte dei popoli*, "Libreria del Littorio" (Roma, 1928).

INTRODUCTION

3. Said hypothesis usually passes unobserved. I have never seen it mentioned by modern authors. It has been set forth explicitly in my articles "Le leggi di evoluzione della popolazione" ("The Laws of Evolution of Population"), *Economia*, December, 1924.

4. In the publications mentioned below we find developed, and often documented, most of the considerations recorded in the following pages.

Il sesso dal punto di vista statistico (Palermo: Remo Sandron, 1908).

"Il diverso accrescimento delle classi sociali e la concentrazione della ricchezza," *Giornale degli economisti*, Ser. II, Vol. XXXVII (January, 1909).

"I presupposti statistici della teoria della cernita naturale," *Rivista italiana di sociologia*, March–April, 1910 (F'lli Bocca).

"Sui fattori demografici dell'evoluzione delle nazioni," *Rivista italiana di sociologia*, 1911.

I fattori demografici dell'evoluzione delle nazioni (Torino: F'lli Bocca, 1912).

"Contributi statistici ai problemi dell'eugenica," *Rivista italiana di sociologia* (Torino: F'lli Bocca), May–August, 1912; translated into English under the title "Contributions of Demography to Eugenics," *Proceedings of the First International Congress of Eugenics* (London, 1912), Vol. II.

L'ammontare e la composizione della ricchezza delle nazioni, "Library of Social Science" (Torino: F'lli Bocca, 1914), Vol. LXII.

"Fattori latenti delle guerre," *Rivista italiana di sociologia*, 1915.

"Fattori demografici delle guerre," *La riforma sociale*, 1915.

"Delle teorie sulle cause delle guerre," Introduction to the book of L. Maroi, *I fattori demografici del conflitto europeo* (Roma: Athenaeum, 1918).

"Teorie sulle cause delle guerre," *Politica*, 1919.

Problemi sociologici della guerra (Bologna: Zanichelli, 1921).

"Le relazioni dell'eugenica con le altre scienze biologiche e sociali," *Atti del Primo Congresso Italiano di Eugenica Sociale, Milano, 20–23 settembre 1924* (Milano: Fondazione Felice Mantovani).

POPULATION

"Le leggi di evoluzione della popolazione," *Economia* (Trieste), December, 1924, No. 12.

"Sul controllo delle nascite," *La difesa sociale* (Roma), Anno IV, Nos. 3–4 (March–April, 1925); translated into English under the title, "On Birth Control," in *Proceedings of the Sixth International Neo-Malthusian and Birth Control Conference* (New York, 1926).

"Decline in the Birth-Rate and the 'Fecundability' of Woman," *Eugenic Review*, January, 1926 (London: Eugenics Education Society).

"Le basi teoriche della politica economica," *Economia* (Trieste), 1926; translated into English under the title "The Theoretical Bases of Economic Policy," *Journal of Political Economy* (Chicago), 1929.

Patologia economica, Università Commerciale Luigi Bocconi, Milano, 1924–1925 (3d ed.; Milano: Tenconi, 1925).

Lezioni di politica economica, R. Università di Roma, 1925–1926; lectures compiled by Dr. M. Carta (Roma: Sampaolesi, 1926).

"Il problema demografico dell'Inghilterra," *Politica* (Roma, 1926).

"Il problema demografico inglese," *Annali di Economia dell'Università Bocconi* (Milano, 1927).

"Les calamités économiques et sociales," *Matériaux pour l'étude des calamités* (Genève, 1926).

"Les mouvements de population," *Revue d'hygiene* (Paris), 1927.

Il neo-organicismo (Catania: Studio editoriale moderno, 1927).

Sociologia, lectures gathered and compiled by F. Lapenna and A. Parboni (Roma: A. Sampaolesi, 1927).

"Considerazioni sull'optimum di densità della popolazione," *Economia* (Trieste, 1927), translated into English under the title "Considerations on the Optimum Density of a Population," *Proceedings of the World Population Conference, 1927* (London, 1927).

"Alcune ricerche italiane sulla produttività differenziale," *Economia*, 1927, translated into English under the title "Some Italian Inquiries into Differential Reproductivity," *Proceedings of the World Population Conference, 1927.*

"La fertilità della donna in relazione al problema della popolazione," *Economia*, 1927.

INTRODUCTION

"Il congresso mondiale della popolazione," *Echi e commenti* (Roma, 1927).

"La natalità e la potenza delle nazioni," *Il popolo di Roma*, January 29, 1920.

"Problemi della popolazione," from the *Annali dell'Istituto di Statistica, Anno Accademico 1927–1928*, Vol. II (Bari: Royal University "Benito Mussolini").

"Le obbiezioni alla politica della crescente natalita," *Archivio fascista di Medicina Politica, Anno II*, Vols. V and VII (September–December, 1928).

La politica della popolazione, stenographic records gathered by Franco Fusillo (Roma: Castellani, 1928).

5. Cf. Plutarco, *Le vite degli uomini illustri* ("*The Lives of Famous Men*"), Vol. VI, *Silla*, 299. Translation by Pompei (Padua: Crescini, 1817).

6. Cf. W. M. Flinders Petrie, *The Revolutions of Civilisation* (3d ed.; London: Harper & Bros., 1922).

7. Oskar Bail, "Untersuchungen über die M-Konzentration von Bakterien und Bakteriophagen, 1924," *Archiv für Hygiene*, XCIV, 54–72; E. Singer and F. Hoder, "Über die physiologische Grenze der Bakterienvermehrung, 1924," *ibid.*, pp. 353–69; Dr. Schokitschi Katzu, "Über die M-Konzentration satzbildender Bakterien, 1924," *ibid.*, XCV, 101–20; O. Bail, "Prolegomena zu einer experimentellen Populationsforschung," *Medizinische Klinik*, Jahr. 1927, No. 1; "Ergebnisse experimenteller Populationsforschung, 1928," *Zeitschrift für Immunitätsforschung*, Bd. LX (1929), Heft 1–2.

8. I refer to the well-known researches of Pearl and his co-operators upon the *Drosophila melanogaster*. A summary of the results obtained by them, together with the bibliographical indications of their publications, can be found in the report, "The Biology of Population Growth," presented by Pearl in 1927 to the World Population Conference at Geneva. See *Proceedings of the World Population Conference* (London: Arnold, 1927), pp. 22–38.

It is known that Pearl maintains that the development of the

Drosophila follows the so-called "logistic" curve introduced by the Belgian mathematician Verhulst in 1838, and then discovered, independently, by Pearl and Reed in 1920 (cf. R. Pearl and L. J. Reed, "On the Mathematical Theory of Population Growth," *Metron*, Vol. III, No. 1). He also maintains that the human populations are developing in accordance with the same curve, a thesis which has aroused much discussion. Among the critics of Pearl, Knibbs should be remembered particularly; his point of view has also been expressed in *Metron* (Vol. V, No. 3) in the article "The Growth of Human Populations and the Laws of Their Increase."

In the discussions which, during the World Population Conference, followed the report by Pearl, Dr. Netusil recalled the researches of Professor Bail (cf. *Proceedings*, pp. 47–48). According to the report of the discussion, Netusil also declared that both the increase and the decrease of the bacterial populations followed the logistic curve; that the course of decrease would be three times longer than that of growth; and that the diminution would be determined at last, not only by the deaths of the bacteria living before but also by an increasing disparity between reproduction and mortality. I do not find these particulars among the articles of Bail above cited, but it is probable that Netusil (now unfortunately deceased, as is also Bail) was fully acquainted with the researches Bail was at that time making and which, as far as I am informed, were not published later.

I.   THE EVOLUTION OF NATIONS

The keystone to an understanding of the evolution of nations is the different rate of increase of the different categories of the population.

The individuals forming a society, like the cells forming an organism, are endowed with very different powers of reproduction. Many die out without descendants; others live through a single child; others multiply themselves with many children. The phenomenon is one commonly observed, but its bearing is not as a rule appreciated. Of the individuals who die out, from two-fifths to two-thirds, according to the period and country, are unmarried; of those who have married, one-third to one-seventh die without descendants. The generation which survives does not, therefore, descend from the whole of the generation which disappears, but only from a fraction thereof which varies, roughly speaking, from a maximum of one-half to a minimum of two-ninths. But the components of this fraction in their turn play a very different part in producing the generation which survives them. It may be said that, with slight variations from country to country, half the generation which survives proceeds from approximately 30 per cent of the married leaving children, and that three-quarters proceed from approximately 60 per cent. We are therefore led to the conclusion that half the generation which survives descends from a very small fraction, varying from one-seventh to one-fifteenth of the generation which is disappearing; while a large majority, amounting to three-fourths of the generation which survives, descends from a still relatively small fraction, varying from one-third to one-eighth per cent of the generation which is disappearing (1).

Now these notable differences in the reproductive powers of different individuals appear to be, to some extent, systematically connected with the social class to which they belong. It may be said that, as a rule, the upper classes are less fertile than the middle, and that these, as a rule, are less so than the lower classes. There are exceptions, to which I shall refer later on, but they do not suffice to offset the rule. Wealth, nobility, culture, high social position, intellectual professions, refinement of life, urbanism, all factors determining the social level, are shown by the many inquiries undertaken to be apparently more or less closely related, but always in a negative sense, with reproductivity (2).

Moreover, their influence is cumulative. Taken as a whole, the upper classes are found to be incapable of maintaining, by their reproductive powers alone, their numerical ratio to the population as a whole; and this insufficiency is more keenly felt during those periods when nations are on an ascending parabola and when consequently the most elevated social positions acquire ever greater importance.

The necessity of avoiding or filling up the gaps thus caused tends to provoke a current from the middle classes to the upper, and from the lower to the middle, a current which is much more important than the opposite current of declassed individuals who fall below their original level (3).

The *demographic metabolism*, as I have called it, thus brought about between the several social classes forming the population is of incalculable importance from many points of view; it explains the disappearance of celebrated families and the need of infusing new blood into the nobility; it tends to accentuate the concentration of wealth; one of its results is that hereditary physical and intellectual characteristics—no less than those relating to culture, religion, language, traditionally handed down in family lineage—tends to spread from the lower strata of society to the whole population, sometimes transforming its racial composition, ideals, and habits, and always keeping the governing classes in close touch with the mass of the people (4).

For the question we are considering, it is of special importance to note that this demographic metabolism differs in intensity and in kind at the various stages of growth of the population, just as occurs with organic metabolism during the successive phases in the growth of an individual (5).

During a first period, when social differentiation is limited and the rate of influence of the upper classes continues high, the rising current is relatively feeble, and anyhow insufficient to afford an outlet to the natural rate of increase of the lower classes, who therefore tend to pour out of the state through wars or emigration. This is the period of national expansion, corresponding to the youthful stage of the individual organism. It is followed by a phase of maturity, when the upper classes, who have become more numerous and whose fertility is reduced, absorb all or almost all the individuals rising from the lower classes, who, in their turn, have lost their most prolific elements through wars or emigration, and whose birth-rate has therefore already declined. The population then attains a state of equilibrium in which it suffices for, or is only slightly in excess of, the needs of the national territory. But as economic disparity increases and the reproductivity of the upper classes declines still farther, the rising current, although it grows, is, on the one hand, found to be insufficient, unless supplemented by immigration, to fill worthily the ever widening gaps left by the governing classes; while on the other hand, the numbers of the lower classes are reduced to an extent which interferes with the proper equilibrium of social functions. The stage is then reached when population declines, a stage corresponding to that of the old age of an individual.

And here an important problem arises: Is this demographic metabolism a phenomenon of an exclusively economic or social nature? or are its roots to be found in more intimate biological factors?

Undoubtedly the economic differentiation of society is partly due to the different degree of fertility of families. Calculations have indeed been made which show what concentration of wealth would result in the course of a generation exclusively as the effect of the different degree of fertility of the parents, supposing they all started equally rich and divided their property among their children in equal portions (6).

But it is no less certain that economic and social differentiation plays a part in determining the different degree of fertility of individuals and in accentuating the consequent demographic metabolism. According to a current opinion, particularly favorable conditions of life have the physiological effect of weakening the reproductive powers of the individual. In the human species physiological factors are, moreover, accentuated by psychological factors, when reason, asserting itself over the impulse of instinct, makes parents reflect on the future of their children. The richer the parents, the more difficult it will be for the children, if they are numerous, to keep up the economic and social standards of the family and to secure for themselves those intellectual and moral satisfactions—*psychic requirements* as they have been called—which people are often more unwilling to relinquish than even food itself (7).

When, moreover, social differentiation becomes sharper and demographic metabolism more active, and it becomes increasingly difficult to rise from the lower to the upper social classes, it is often found necessary to delay marriage or to limit the number of the children in order to make such a rise possible, so that the new additions no longer bring to the higher classes the contribution of large families, and those who aspire to enter those classes limit, in the meantime, their offspring.

These considerations explain certain exceptions or qualifications to the rule of the different rate of growth of the social classes. In England, during the period of great industrial expansion, the wide horizons opened to the governing classes removed the psychic restraint placed on reproduction, while the low standard of living of the working classes increased their death-rate; and we can thus understand how it was that the rate of increase of the upper classes was much less below that of the lower classes than it came to be later on (8).

The desire to improve one's social position, which the war and post-war agitations have left in the masses, explains why their natural rate of increase has fallen off considerably, falling perhaps in some countries even below that of the upper classes (9).

But very probably that economic and demographic differentiation which accompanies the evolution of nations, and the social metabolism to which it gives rise, are, fundamentally, common manifestations of more intimate biological factors (10). It has often been remarked that the upper classes precede the evolution of the nations to which they belong. Now this fact, which is generally observed in relation to phenomena of a psychic and moral order, is ascribed to the influence which the governing classes exercise over the rest of population through example and legislation; but it also seems to hold good for physical characteristics from which all direct influence of compulsion, or education, or imitation, must be excluded (11). Now it is only natural that, just as the several races, groups, and nations describe, so likewise do different families describe, at different rates of speed, the parabola of evolution. The more precocious families, which precede the mass in the evolution of their germs, would thus raise themselves above the others and form the backbone of the governing classes; but they would subsequently present, sooner than the others, the organic symptoms of decay.

This would explain why the upper classes, when isolated, end by degenerating, however conspicuous may have been the endowments of the original heads of the families.

This would also explain how it is that while the upper classes are less prolific than the lower, yet the less capable individuals belonging to the upper classes are the least prolific, as recent researches point out (12). The explanation is that in the descending part of the parabola of evolution declining reproductivity is accompanied, from a certain stage onward, by a decline also in the qualities of the individual.

The ideas above set forth throw new light on the phenomenon of the different rate of growth of the social classes, which has led many students in the past to fear progressive decline in the quality of the nations. On the contrary, we now see it is a providential mechanism for the elimination of those family stocks which have fulfilled the cycle of their evolution. To hope to improve the race by artificially stimulating the fertility of the upper classes is a delusion comparable to that of those who should hope to increase the efficiency of the population by prolonging artificially the life of the aged (13).

And again, influence exerted by psychic requirements, which makes the wealthy and upper classes desire small families, is seen to be a wise provision by which nature reconciles psychic tendencies with the physiological capacities of those classes who have advanced farthest along the parabola of their evolution.

In other words, the lower birth-rate of the upper classes is not fundamentally due to Neo-Malthusian theories. It is rather the fact that the urge of genetic instincts has ceased, which allows their minds to receive the persuasive arguments of reason in favor of regulating the number of their children, and so makes them content with families which are of necessity small, and gives them the illusion that they do not desire that which they could not obtain without forcing nature. In the same way the individual, as he grows older, finds many reasons to be satisfied with that orderly and well-regulated life which his years would in any case compel him to live, reasons which had no hold over him when in the fulness of his powers, but which alone enable him now to watch, without undue regret, the gradual decline of the flame of life (16).

We must therefore conclude that the primary cause of the evolution of nations must be sought in biological factors. A smaller or larger ratio of the family stocks which have proceeded farthest along the parabola of evolution characterizes, in substance, the successive stages in the evolution of nations.

This would explain the opposite effects produced by the same causes on populations at different stages of their evolution.

Unemployment, which is now considered one of the reasons for the declining birth-rate (15), was, according to the evidence afforded by all the documents of the period, one of the causes of the unusual frequency of marriages and births which led to the well-known overpopulation crisis in Ireland in the first half of the nineteenth century (16).

Another factor which then was said to contribute to that high birth-rate was the minute subdivision of land (17); whereas it is well known that the subdivision of landed property, facilitated by the succession laws of the Napoleonic Code, is regarded as one of the causes of the widespread limitation of births among the French (18).

But of late years it is not in France or in countries where similar laws regulate inheritance that the lowest birth-rates are found, but in countries governed by opposite principles, such as England and Sweden (19). This can be ascribed to the growing importance taken in late years by the desire of keeping up one's own social position, still more than to that of preserving the property for a child, as an influence determining the limitation of the birth-rate. This desire leads those children who are not favored by the succession laws to avoid marriage or the begetting of children even more frequently than would have been the case under a system providing for the subdivision of the family estate (20).

Thus, also, the grants made to families based on the number of children, which in an age when the birth-rate is generally rationalized would seemingly exercise a stimulating influence, have shown themselves under other circumstances to be not only useless but injurious to the birth-rate, a fact which can be explained by the consideration that they awaken or develop in families the restricting influence of psychic requirements (21).

High infant mortality, which in vigorously expanding populations is constantly associated with a high birth-rate (22), becomes among dying populations a further reason for refusing to propagate (23).

The biological theory of the evolution of nations also explains why the rise, the arrest, and the fall of population are either accompanied or followed at no great distance, by the expansion, the stoppage, or the decline of other national manifestations in the military, economic, political, and scientific fields. The fact is that those same genetic forces which determine a rapid growth of the population cause at the same time a notable flowering of robust and daring individuals of keen, prompt, and adaptable intelligence.

All these circumstances contribute to determine the golden age of a nation. It is no mere chance, therefore, that in periods of rapidly expanding population the nations find the great captains who lead them to victory, the industrial geniuses who provide them with the arms required for the needs of war and peace, the great poets who idealize their aspirations and electrify their enthusiasm, the great thinkers who systematize their conceptions of life and of the universe, and the great historians who transmit their deeds to posterity (24).

To these genetic factors must be added a purely demographic factor, dependent on the age-composition of the population. For, when a nation is in a period of expanding birth-rate, the population is rich in young people; whereas, when a nation advances in the phase of demographic decline, the opposite phenomenon occurs, and the older age groups acquire increasing importance. This has a decisive effect on the psychology of the nation, for a population in which young age-groups abound bears the imprint of their spirit of daring in all its social organization and in the trend of its collective policies; whereas cold, calculating prudence is the characteristic of populations in which the older age-groups prevail (25).

A secret harmony is thus revealed between the numerical increase and the intellectual development, between the physical characteristics and the age-group composition of a people, and between its spirit of initiative and the demographic conditions which secure to that initiative the chances of success.

We can note a similar harmony in the growth of the individual organism. If this harmony generally passes unnoticed, it is only because it is so general that it is looked upon as obvious. As a matter of fact, it is indeed wonderful to note that at the same age at which the intellect attains its greatest vigor and plasticity, physical strength also attains the zenith of power and endurance, and that confidence in the future and daring in conceiving and carrying out projects correspond to that stage of life in which the power of the intellect and the strength of the body are asserting themselves and progressing; whereas reflection and circumspection, and, later on, timidity, characterize the last years of adult life and old age, and coincide with the progressive exhaustion of the physical and intellectual faculties (26).

All this teaches us the lesson that a thorough study of the functioning of the machinery of the evolution of nations shows that nature has indeed provided much better than many of the theorists on population have thought and think, when they wish to replace natural processes by artificial rationalization (27).

The lesson is similar to that which in other times was taught by the study of human physiology. For a long time doctors who devoted their attention to the human organism, impressed by the disturbances to which it is subject in the crises of growth and in diseases, thought they could correct nature by drastic remedies which would compel the organism to return to its normal equilibrium. Only subsequently, as the result of more thorough examination, have they been forced to recognize that in reality the processes of nature are based on intimate and profound reasons, and that, in trying to replace them by artificial devices, the loss is often much greater than the gain, so that the wisest course is still, in most cases, that of not hindering but of facilitating and assisting their work (28).

Of course, this does not mean that natural processes do not sometimes offer serious drawbacks.

As far as social metabolism is concerned, there is no doubt that its intensification, more especially when marked differentiation reduces the fertility of those who rise or who hope to rise, hastens the demographic exhaustion of the nation. It is also certain that when the social metabolism becomes too rapid and intense, the individuals who rise to the upper classes are often lacking in that intellectual and moral preparation for occupying positions of responsibility which can only be supplied by a long family tradition (29).

This explains why at certain stages in the evolution of nations an effort has been made to curb and sometimes to prevent demographic interchanges between the several social classes. The caste system represents the strictest enforcement of this program. This system removes, on the one hand, the stimulus to reduce the birth-rate which comes from the desire to ascend; on the other hand, it determines a high demand for the directing functions of society, which tends to raise the remuneration assigned to the upper classes and to reduce, in their case, the economic stimulus to rationalize births. In the lower classes, who are cut off from an outlet upward, the result is a superabundant birth-rate, which cannot fail to deteriorate the standard of life and which, by raising the death-rate, limits their natural increase.

Undoubtedly the caste system delays the evolution of a nation. And this may, from certain points of view, be considered advantageous. But, on the other hand, the upper classes, deprived of the infusion of new blood from the mass of the population, crystallize in antiquated, traditional ideas and often degenerate both physically and intellectually, so that civilization remains stationary or progresses less rapidly.

The consequent lack of qualitative and quantitative equilibrium between the upper and lower classes often leads to the overthrow, by peaceful or violent means, of the barriers and to a return to the system of free social circulation. This is what occurred in Rome as a result of the struggle between patricians and plebeians; this is what occurred, on a larger scale, with the French Revolution (30).

On other occasions the defects of the system of free circulation between the classes leads to a return to the system of exclusiveness, as was the case in Venice when admission of new families to the Grand Council was closed.

It thus seems that we are faced by alternative systems of social organization, one of which leads the nations to a briefer but more intense life, the other to a long and peaceful one. Vigor of life and duration of life thus seem to be mutually exclusive, at least in the case of nations.

The latter system is that generally prevailing in ancient civilizations, and which until recently prevailed in oriental civilizations, and has not yet disappeared; the former is the system characteristic of Western European civilization and of the new countries to which it has given rise. The superiority of white civilization in modern times seems indeed to bear witness in favor of the former system, and seems to show that again in this field the devices of man prove themselves inferior to the machinery provided by nature; and the growing adoption by the oriental civilizations of the European and

American system of social organization may rightly be interpreted as a recognition of this superiority.

We may repeat for the nations a motto which comes down to us from no other than an Eastern monarch, "Better live one day as a lion than a hundred years as a sheep."

NOTES

1. For the data corresponding to the single states, see *I fattori demografici dell'evoluzione delle nazioni* (Torino: F'lli Bocca, 1912), pp. 9–12.

2. The results of researches made in the last years, by me and by other Italian authors (Savorgnan, Mortara, Giusti, and Luzzatto Fegiz) in this field are summarized in the article "Alcune ricerche sulla riproduttività differenziale" published in Italian in *Economia* and in English in *Proceedings of the World Population Conference* (1927). I must, however, state that the English translation, published without my authorization before the proofs were corrected, contains several mistakes, which, *inter alia*, make the formula of average reproductive power incomprehensible. The said article gives the related bibliography up to date. In the acts of the same Congress are published the memoranda presented by Carr-Saunders, March, Grotjahn, and Methorst, presenting data on the subject for their respective countries. For the United States of America, Pearl has published some data in the *Quarterly Review of Biology* ("Differential Fertility," March, 1927), Ogburn in *Social Forces* ("Birth Rates and Social Classes," September, 1929), and Sydenstricker in the *Public Health Reports* ("Differential Fertility According to Economic Status," August 30, 1929). For Hungary, and particularly for Budapest, see the data given by Bela Foeldes in the *Journal de la Société Hongroise de Statistique* ("Influence de la situation matérielle et sociale sur les mariages, les naissances et les décès, eu égard particulièrement à Budapest" ["Influence of the Material and Social Situation upon Marriages, Births, and

Deaths, Particularly as Regards Budapest"] (1929, Nos. 1–2). Foeldes cites, and often reprints, numerous data obtained for the various countries by other authors.

At the said Congress were also presented two papers, one by Professor Aznar of Madrid and the other by Dr. Edin of Stockholm, which were summarized in the *Proceedings* and which later on formed the object of the following memoranda by the authors. Dr. Edin's memorandum "Fertility in Marriage in the Different Social Classes of Greater Stockholm in the Years 1919–1922," was distributed in manuscript. The one of Professor Aznar, "El promedio diferencial de la reproductividad in las clases sociales de Madrid," was published in the first number, January, 1929, of the *Boletin de la Universidad de Madrid*. These two articles are particularly interesting as they would show that the net productivity of the marriages (average number of the children living per marriage) is higher in the richer classes.

This result, however, is not sufficient to justify the assertion that reproductivity is higher in the wealthier classes, because, apart from illegitimate births, the reproductivity depends not only on the net productivity of marriages but also upon the probability of marriage and the average duration of a generation (average age of the parents at the birth of the children). Reproductivity is indeed a positive function of the probability of marriage and a negative function of the duration of a generation. Now, it is known that the probability of marriage is higher and the age at marriage lower in the lower classes. The influence of the probability of marriage upon reproductivity has been indicated by Aznar (*op. cit.*, pp. 6–7, n.), while I do not remember to have seen due notice taken of the influence of the duration of a generation.

The same observations diminish the value of other inquiries pointing to the high productivity of marriages in the upper classes, as indicating a lower degree of growth in the lower strata of the population. On the bases of documents showing the taxes paid in the eighteenth century in the city of Castellamare di Stabia (Naples), Dr. D. de Meo ascertained that the number of living children was on the average higher for heads of property-owning families than for the propertyless (the average age of the heads of property-owning families was, however, higher, and so was the frequency of bachelors) (*Distribuzione della ricchezza e composizione demografica in alcune città dell'Italia meridionale nel secolo XVIII* ["*The Distribution of Wealth and the Composition of the Population in Some Cities of the South of Italy during the XVIII Century*"], Regio Istituto Superiore di Scienze Economiche e Commerciali [High School of Commerce], Naples, 1927–28). In China Griffing has found that the families of literate people as compared to those of the unlettered, and the families of the better-educated country people as compared to those of the less-educated, present on the average more living births, fewer infantile deaths, and more surviving children (J. B. Griffing, "Education and Size of Family in China," *Journal of Heredity*, September, 1926, pp. 331–37).

3. For the relative importance of the ascending and descending current in the various countries, see *The Demographic Factors in the Evolution of the Nations* (*I fattori demografici dell'evoluzione delle nazioni*), note on pp. 25, 29, and *The Amount and Composition of the Wealth of the Nations* (*L'ammontare e la composizione della ricchezza delle nazioni*), p. 428. To the points therein quoted I can add some others taken from an inquiry made by the General Direction of Statistics of Italy on students entered in the rolls of the universities and commercial high schools during the academic year of 1912. For 9,686 students the inquiry stated the profession of the father, showing that three-fourths or more of the students come from the upper classes (liberal professions and property-owners) and one-fourth from the lower classes, of whom 14 per cent, or a little under, are from the lower middle class (clerks, shopkeepers, and artists), 7 per cent from skilled workmen, and 4 per cent from the unskilled workmen.

The comparison between these data and those published in the passage of *The Demographic Factors, etc.*, quoted above, concerning men married in Rome in 1908 show, as might have been expected, that the percentage pertaining to the upper classes, who had risen from the lower classes, was considerably higher in Rome than in the kingdom as a whole. Of the 819 bridegrooms pertaining to the higher classes (classified on the same principle adopted in classifying the fathers of the students), only 61 per cent originally came from those classes, 14 per cent came from the class of small employees, shop-keepers, and artists, 18 per cent from the class of skilled workers, and 7 per cent from that of unskilled workers. In Sweden, the percentage of the students in the universities and in the high schools coming from the lower classes is much higher: 51.6 per cent for the students of the University of Lund; 63.7 per cent (1885) and 60.4 per cent (1897) for the students of the high schools (see *Demographic Factors, etc.*, pp. 25–26). The comparison between the data for the different countries is, however, very difficult to make, owing to the different principles adopted in classifying professional and social categories. This consideration withheld me from publishing interesting data communicated to me by Professor Vincenzo Castrilli, of the Royal University of Bari, concerning the universities of Prussia and Hungary. From these it appears, however, evident that the percentage of students coming from the lower classes is in Hungary (1925–26) lower, and in Prussia, both before and since the war, much higher than in Italy in 1911–12. For Prussia the comparison of the pre-war data (summer of 1911 and winter 1911–12) with the post-war data (winter 1924–25, summer 1925, summer 1928) show a small but constant decrease in the percentage of students coming from the higher classes; it shows also a heavy decline in the percentage of students coming from the middle classes during the summer 1924–25 in comparison to the pre-war period, followed by an increase from 1924–25 to 1928, which, however, does not bring the percentage up to the previous level. To secure on this subject comparable international statistics for the different states is one of the objects which the International Commission of Intellectual Statistics has in view.

4. Cf., more particularly, the works quoted: *The Different Growth of Social Classes* (*Il diverso accrescimento delle classi sociali*), pp. 61–69; *The Demographic Factors in the Evolution of the Nations* (*I fattori demografici dell'evoluzione delle nazioni*), pp. 4–12, 30–34; "Contributions of Demography to Eugenics" ("Contributi statistici ai problemi dell'eu-

genica"), pp. 378–83; "Latent Factors of War" ("Fattori latenti della guerra"); "Theories upon the Causes of War" ("Teorie sulle cause della guerra"); "The Laws of Evolution of Populations" ("Le leggi di evoluzione della popolazione"), p. 294; *The Amount and Composition of the Wealth of the Nations* (*L'ammontare e la camposizione della ricchezza delle nazioni*), pp. 429–31.

5. Cf. particularly: *The Demographic Factors in the Evolution of the Nations* (*I fattori demografici della evoluzione delle nazioni*), pp. 34–47; "Contributions of Demography to Eugenics" ("Contributi statistici ai problemi dell'eugenica"), p. 380; "Latent Factors of War" ("Fattori latenti della guerre"); *The Amount and Composition, etc.* (*L'ammontare e la composizione ecc.*), pp. 367–431; "The Laws of Evolution of Populations" ("Le eggi di evoluzione della popolazione"), pp. 285–86.

6. Cf. "Indexes of Concentration and of Dependence" ("Indici di concentrazione e di dipendenza") in *Biblioteca dell'economista*, Ser. V, Vol. XX, pp. 78–79, and "On the Measurement of Concentration and Variability of the Characters" ("Sulla misura della concentrazione e della variabilità dei caratteri") in the *Atti del R. Istituto Veneto di Scienze, Lettere e Arti 1913–1914*, LXXIII, Part II, 1223–25.

7. See particularly "The Laws of Evolution of Populations" ("Le leggi di evoluzione della popolazione"), p. 284, and *Economic Pathology (Patologia economica)* pp. 4–8.

8. For data and discussion on this subject, see K. Pearson, "On the Inheritance of the Mental and Moral Characters in Man" in *Biometrica*, March and July, 1904, pp. 159–60; D. Heron, *On the relation of Fertility in Man to Social Status and on the Changes in the Relation That Have Taken Place during the Last Fifty Years* (London: Dulau & Co., 1906); A. Newsholme and T. H. C. Stevenson, "The Decline of Human Fertility in the United Kingdom and Other Countries, as Shown by Corrected Birth Rates," *Journal of the Royal Statistics Society*, March, 1906, p. 66; G. U. Yule, "On the Changes in the Marriage and Birth Rates in England and Wales, etc.," *ibid.*, pp. 118–21; C. Gini, *Il diverso accrescimento ecc.*, art. cited, Part. IX; T. H. C.

Stevenson, "The Fertility of Various Classes in England and Wales from the Middle of the Nineteenth Century to 1911," *Journal of the Royal Statistics Society*, pp. 417–18. The data given by Stevenson show that the marriages contracted during the period 1851–61 and 1861–71 registered in the census of 1911 indicate a less-marked difference in the fertility of the various social classes than do the marriages contracted in the successive periods. He, however, failed to point out in this connection that the longer the duration of the marriages returned, the younger the ages of the spouses must have been; and the difference, from this point of view, between the various social classes must have been less. Now it is known that the different degree of fertility of the various social classes depends to a great extent on the difference of age at which marriages are contracted. One can literally repeat, in this connection, what Stevenson observes a few pages later on (p. 425) with regard to another question: "It is necessary to be cautious in accepting this apparent increase, because the effect of mortality alone, as we work back towards a period from which the youngest brides alone can survive, must be to approximate all surviving marriages towards a common level of earliness." It is, therefore, more than likely that toward the middle of the century the differences were greater than would appear from the data of Stevenson; but it seems, on the other hand, that the differences were then less than in the pre-war years. This is very likely due in part to the circumstance referred to in the text: it was also probably due in part to the fact that births began to decline in the upper classes, who generally precede the others, as I observed in the above-mentioned article. Stevenson lays stress exclusively upon this last circumstance and in his turn ascribes the decline of the birth-rate to the spread of Neo-Malthusian practices. Even accepting this explanation, nothing justifies the suggestion of Stevenson (p. 417) that, if the comparison were placed another 20 years back, no sensible difference in the fertility of the various social classes would be found. In fact, since he admits that the influence of the Neo-Malthusian campaign began to be felt in 1877, he should have come to the conclusion that before this date the differences in the fertility of the various social classes represented a static condition.

9. See the significant data for some towns of Germany reported by Professor Grotjahn in the report, "Differential Birth Rate in Germany," presented to the World Congress of Population in Geneva. Cf. *Proceedings*, pp. 153–54, and, bearing in mind the above reservations (cf. note 2), the results of the researches of Dr. Edin for Stockholm.

10. This theory was set forth in the paper "Contributions of Demography to Eugenics" presented to the First International Congress of Eugenics (London, 1912). (Cf. Vol. II of the *Proceedings*, where the paper was printed in the English translation; the Italian text was published in the *Rivista italiana di sociologia* under the title of "Contributi statistici ai problemi dell'eugenica," May–August, 1912, and developed later in the report on "The Relations of Eugenics to the Other Branches of Biological and Social Sciences" ("Le relazioni dell'eugenica con le altre scienze biologiche e sociali") presented to the first Italian Congress of Eugenics (1924); in the lecture on "The Laws of Evolution of Populations ("Le leggi di evoluzione della popolazione") held in the same year at Brescia; in the article "Decline in the Birth Rate and Fecundability of Woman" (*Eugenic Review*, January, 1926); and more especially in the lectures upon "Population Policies" ("La politica della popolazione") held at the University of Rome during the academic year 1927–28.

11. I may quote in this connection Professor V. Giuffrida Ruggeri, who thinks that in all the human races there is a tendency to the refinement of the physical type and who in this refinement recognizes an *orthogenesis* characteristic of the human species ("Incroci ai due estremi della gerarchia delle razze umane," *Rivirta d'Italia*, July, 1910, p. 173). See also the interesting remarks made by F. A. Woods (*Mental and Moral Heredity in Royalty* [New York, 1926]) and by A. E. Wiggam (*The Fruit of the Family Tree* [London: T. Werner Laurie, Ltd., 1925]) upon the variations of facial characteristics as shown by portraits of members of the royal families and of the upper classes in Northern

Europe from the fifteenth to the eighteenth century. Very frequently in the fifteenth century their faces were of the coarse type—"bovine," as these authors say—such as one now meets only in the lower classes of those countries, making one think that the typical aspect of the highest classes of Northern Europe in the successive centuries evolved toward that finer type (called by the authors "Greek" and which might better be called "classic"), a type which already prevailed in South Italy. Dr. Woods maintains that this evolution has taken place through the spread in the northern countries of the aesthetic, classical ideal and the consequent selection through marriage which has taken place in this sense; but in truth it seems difficult to attribute to selection through marriage so great an influence in so short a time. On the other hand, nobody can deny that the classic type is found today with a certain frequency also in the lower classes of Northern Europe, whereas in Southern Europe this classic type has long prevailed, especially in such districts as Venice, whose population lives in a condition of relative segregation. According to these facts, we must conclude that in this evolution of the type, the upper classes in the northern countries have only preceded the lower, repeating probably a phenomenon which had already taken place in the South, with its older civilization.

12. F. A. Woods, "Aristocracies and Mental Evolution of Social 'conification,'" *Metron*, Vol. VII, No. 3 (1928).

13. See, to this effect, "Contributions of Demography to Eugenics" ("Contributi statistici ai problemi dell'eugenica"), p. 383; "The Relation of Eugenics to the Other Branches of Biological and Social Science" ("Le relazioni dell'eugenica con le altre scienze biologische e sociali"), p. 17; "The Laws of Evolution of Population" ("Le leggi di evoluzione della popolazione"), p. 294; "Some Italian Inquiries into Differential Reproductivity" ("Alcune ricerche italiane sulla produttività differenziale"), pp. 75–79 of the reprint; "Population Policies" ("La politica della popolazione"), pp. 96–97.

14. See "The Laws of Evolution of Population" ("Le leggi di evoluzione della popolazione"), p. 286, and the lectures on the "Popu-

lation Policies" ("La politica della popolazione") and the paper upon "The Fertility of Woman in Relation to the Problem of Population" ("La fertilità della donna in relazione al problema della popolazione") held at the World Population Congress at Geneva and published in *Economia*. Of this paper, the *Proceedings* contain only a résumé not revised by me, full of errors which in several points change, and in some cases completely invert, my thought.

The affirmation that the adoption, on a large scale, of Neo-Malthusian practices is fundamentally due to a weakening of the genetic instinct may be unwelcome to those belonging to nations with whom this practice is general, and for this reason it will certainly be received with a certain degree of incredulity. The incredulous will do well to read the volume, *A Research in Marriage* (New York: Boni, 1929), wherein Dr. G. V. Hamilton reports the results of a detailed and accurate research conducted by him upon the sexual life of 200 intellectual families of New York made at the request and at the expense of a scientific committee. No less than 46 of the 100 women examined were found inadequate to complete the sexual act (cf. 542). Contraceptive practices were followed by 87 per cent of the women, no doubt a higher percentage than in the general population. The 100 women had 228 pregnancies and 161 children (p. 134). Of the 100 women, 31, and of the 100 men, 33, had sexual relations with the spouse before marriage. Only 29 of the remaining 67 bridegrooms and 28 of the remaining 69 brides had sexual relations on the first night of marriage. Excluding 8 bridegrooms and 11 brides for whom justification was found in various circumstances (separation immediately after marriage, menstruation, pregnancies, sickness), of 59 bridegrooms there remain 30, and of 58 brides, also 30—that is more than 50 per cent—who could not or did not wish to have any intercourse during the first night of marriage (Table 301, pp. 370–71). For England, Dr. Marie Stopes tells that the undersexed types are frequent in the clergy, among teachers and other intellectual classes (cf. *The First Five Thousand, The First Report of the First British Birth Control Clinic*, [London: Bale, 1925], pp. 48–49).

15. For the case of Italy, for instance, this opinion was publicly expressed by Paolo Orano in *Il lavoro d'Italia* ("The Italians That Are to Be Born" ["Gli italiani che devono nascere], September 12, 1928), but in private it is expressed by many.

16. Griffith quotes from the *Reports on the State of the Poor in Ireland, 1830* (p. 351) a passage wherein it is clearly stated that if the men were not "idle and unemployed . . . . they would not be so fond of getting married . . . . the great cause of these intermarriages is idleness, and forming that kind of connections in the winter season; want of employment makes them really get married in many cases" (G. Talbot Griffith, *Population Problems of the Age of Malthus* [Cambridge University Press, 1926], p. 54).

17. Griffith, following in the footsteps of Wakefield (Edward Wakefield, *Account of Ireland* [1812]), maintains that one of the principal causes of the extraordinary increase in the Irish population was "the minute subdivision of land" (*ibid.*, p. 51). Further, on page 58, he states: "The two main causes of the increase of the population . . . . the supply of food and the frequency of marriages, were rendered more effective and a greater menace by the minute subdivision of land, with which for various reasons they were associated." Several passages of the reports of 1825 contain evidence in this regard. The explanation is found by Griffith in the fact that ownership of land "gives to the holder a feeling of power and independence" often misleading.

18. On the occasion of the reform of the Italian Civil Code a special commission was formed by the Minister of Justice to suggest a reform which could increase the birth-rate or eliminate the limitation of births. Among the proposals of the commission was that of modifying the inheritance laws so as to avoid the division of landed property between the descendants. The commission had in mind in making this proposal the results of some inquiries made by Professor Livio Livi presented to the commission and then published in *Economia*, "Researches upon the Birth Rate in Relation to the Types of Agricultural Leases and to the Subdivision of Landed Property" ("In-

[43]

dagini sulla natalità in rapporto ai tipi di contratto agricolo dominanti ed al frazionamento della proprietà terriera"), October, 1927. Livi concluded that in the zones where landed property has been greatly subdivided—i.e., where the holdings areas registered for purposes of the land tax are smallest—the birth-rate is lower and rises as the subdivision declines, up to a certain limit. A revision of Livis calculations and the adoption of more suitable territorial units (the districts and municipalities instead of provinces studied by Livi) have, however, led the Central Institute of Statistics to conclude that no regular connection can be detected between birth- and death-rates and the subdivision of landed property, inasmuch as the variations in the aforesaid rates in accordance with the average size of holdings in the land tax register are either negligible or irregular. The first results of the detailed researches on this matter made by the Central Institute of Statistics were published in the *Notiziario demografico* of December 1, 1928, "Relation between Land Property and Movement of Population ("Rapporto fra proprietà fondiaria e movimento della popolazione"), pp. 5-9.

19. During recent years (1927 and 1928) six states—Sweden, England and Wales, Switzerland, Austria, Estonia, and Norway (in 1928) presented a lower birth-rate than France.

STATE	LIVING BIRTHS PER 1,000 INHABITANTS	
	1927	1928
France	18.1	18.2
Norway	18.2	18.0
Esthonia	17.7	17.7
Austria	17.8	17.5
Switzerland	17.4	17.5
England and Wales	16.6	16.7
Sweden	16.1	16.2

Now, in none of these six countries is the Code Napoléon in force.

20. In speaking on the "Connections between the Demographic and the Economic Evolution of Nations" ("Nessi tra evoluzione

demografica ed evoluzione economica delle Nazioni") at the first of a course of lectures on economic culture held during 1928 at the High School of Commerce at Turin, I noted four stages in demographic evolution linked with the different psychological attitude of the parents as regards production and savings, and corresponding probably to an evolution in the strength of the reproductive instinct. There is a first stage, in which the strength of the instinct is such that even the more wealthy classes give it free scope regardless of the fact that large families will reduce the amount of the property which each child will inherit. This is the stage through which many new countries pass in the early days of immigration, and which was perhaps experienced in some European countries during the period of their greatest industrial prosperity toward the middle of last century. In the second stage the reproductive instinct is not strong enough to make parents indifferent to the more or less advantageous conditions in which their children will be left in accordance with their number, so that the property-owning classes tend to have a smaller number of children, whereas the instinct of reproduction still has full play in the case of the property-less classes. This is the stage reached in most European countries during the latter part of last and the first years of this century. In a third stage, which France already entered sometime ago, followed since the war by many European countries, the reproductive instinct seems so enfeebled that it is not only overcome by considerations of family advantage but also by those of the personal convenience of the parents, leading to a tendency on the part of the lower classes, to limit their offspring, thus removing a powerful stimulus to produce and accumulate wealth. Finally a fourth stage is reached when—probably as a consequence of the natural solidarity which binds the instincts against the sway of reason so that when reason gets the upper hand, they surrender their power one after the other—even the instinct to save and accumulate loses its hold, and the parents not only produce and save less as the number of children to be brought up is reduced but they take less care to preserve and increase inherited wealth, so that at last not only total wealth but also the average per capita wealth declines.

POPULATION

21. Grants are often made to encourage large families, as it is thought that they will assist in meeting the cost of bringing up children and therefore reduce the tendency to birth-control. It is well known that this was the motive in France and New Zealand. But the amount of the grants hitherto made only meets a very small percentage of the expense, and it may lead families, who formerly allowed instinct to guide reproduction, to consider the economic aspects of large families. To this fact, rather than to the direct influence of a higher standard of life brought about by the grants, we must, I believe, look for the explanation of the depressing effect that these grants have sometimes had on the birth-rate. Discussions of the probable effects of grants on the birth-rate are very numerous: I will only mention J. B. Richardson, "The Family Allowances System," *Economic Journal*, September, 1924; R. M. Campbell, "Family Allowances in New Zealand," *ibid.*, September, 1927; E. R. Rathbone, *The Ethics and Economics of Family Endowment* (London: J. A. Sharp, 1927). Researches based on statistics regarding the effects that the system of allowances has really had are very few: I know only one for the Speenhamland system, practiced in a part of England from 1795 to 1834. Cf. J. S. Blackmore and F. C. Mellonie, "Family Endowment and the Birth Rate in the Early Nineteenth Century," *Economic Journal*, Supplement, *Economic History*, No. 2, May, 1927, apart from the data on the French *caisses de compensation* (cf. more particularly the "Résumé du rapport, de M. Ambroise Rendu, conseiller municipal de Paris, président du Comité pour le retour à la terre, sur les Allocations familiales et la natalité," presented at the Huitième Congrès National del a Natalité, Paris, September, 1926, pages 96–97 in the proceedings of the Congress; the "Résumé du rapport, presenté par M. Bonvoisin—directeur du Comité Central des Allocations Familiales sur le Fonctionnement des Caisses de Compensation") at the subsequent Congress held at Tours (1927), pages 101–5 of the *Proceedings;* the report of Colonel Guillermin upon the "Inquiry into the *Caisses de Compensation*, Their Social Work and Influence on the Birth-Rate in Working-Class Families" ("L'enquête sur les caisses de

compensation, leurs œuvres sociales et leur influence sur la natalité ouvrière"), presented at the Eighth National Congress for Family Allowances (Lyon, May 14–17, 1928), pages 55–62 of the *Proceedings*), and the report presented at the same congress by M. Bonvoisin, *Upon the Activity of the Caisses de Compensation in 1927* (*L'activité des caisses de compensation en 1927*), pp. 131 ff.

It would appear that in families affiliated to the caisses de compensation the birth-rate increased sensibly (the numbers given by the several reporters do not, however, coincide), but, as Bonvoisin himself stated at the congress at Toulouse, "perhaps we should only see one of the sides of the attraction which the allowances of these *caisses* have for the families" ("peut être ne faut il voir qu'une des manifestations de l'attrait que présentent, pour les familles, les prestations des caisses" (p. 103). It is certainly probable that the composition of the affiliated families varied over a period of years as regards the duration of the marriages and social position. This circumstance is given by Guillermin as an explanation of the decline of the average number of children in the families receiving allowances verified in 1927 as compared to the two previous years (p. 56) and also by Bonvoisin (*Proceedings of the Congress of Lyon*, pp. 135–36) for the increase in the number of stillborn and the higher infant mortality; but it may also be that this same circumstance may have determined, or contributed to determine, the increase noted in the birth-rate. On the other hand, it appears that in England the system of allowances was accompanied, in the districts where the Speenhamland system was adopted, by a decline and not by an increase of the birth-rate. It may, of course, be that even when it lends to no increase or even when it lends to a decline of the birth-rate, the allowance system may determine a decline in the death-rate. The two English authors above mentioned express the opinion that in England the allowance system reduced infant mortality and that the lower birth-rate was only due to the survival of a larger number of children, which makes parents less desirous of other offspring.

22. This happens not only because a high birth-rate is accompa-

POPULATION

nied by a shorter interval between confinements, which reduces the
strength of the infants and reduces also the care bestowed on them by
their parents (cf. "Contributions of Demography to Eugenics"
["Contributi statistici ai problemi dell'eugenica"], pp. 344–45), but
also because the loss of a child soon after birth makes the parents desire to fill the empty place left in the family and places the mother in
a condition to become pregnant sooner. Upon the shorter interval
between subsequent confinements when the first child has died, cf. the
researches of J. V. Goehlert, *Statistical Researches on Marriages (Sta-
tistische Untersuchungen über die Ehen)* (Wien, 1870), and A. Geissler,
"The Influence of Infantile Mortality on Nuptial Fertility (Über den
Einfluss der Säuglingssterblichkeit auf die eheliche Fruchtbarkeit"),
Zeitschrift des K. Seachsischen Statistischen Bureaus, 1885.

23. Dr. J. R. Baker writes as follows about the population of the
Island of Espiritu Santo: "The people think it useless to produce
children, who will only die in epidemics. . . . . The state of affairs was
very clearly put to me by a native woman on another island. When
I questioned her about the recent death in her villages, she indicated
all the children who were sitting round about her and said: 'Close up
all piccaninny here é die finish' ("all these children will die soon").
This feeling, that it is useless to produce children who will only die, is,
I believe, the cause of the small families in Santo" ("Depopulation in
Espiritu Santo, New Hebrides," *Journal of the Anthropological Institute,* January–June, 1928, pp. 291–92).

24. See "The Laws of Evolution of Nations" ("Le leggi di evoluzione delle nazioni"), p. 292; "The Theoretical Bases of Economic
Policy" ("Le basi teoriche della politica economica"), p. 131.

25. Cf. *The Demographic Factors in the Evolution of Nations
(I fattori demografici dell'evoluzione delle nazioni)*, pp. 37–40, 70–71;
"Latent Factors of War" ("Fattori latenti della guerra"), p. 13;
Population Policies (La politica della popolazione), p. 180.

26. "The Laws of Evolutions of Nations" ("Le leggi di evoluzione delle nazioni"), p. 292; *Population Policies (La politica della
popolazione)*, p. 181.

27. Cf. *Population Policies* (*La politica della popolazione*).

28. Cf. "The Theoretical Bases of Economic Policy" ("Le basi teoriche della politica economica"), p. 143; *Population Policies* (*La politica della popolazione*), pp. 131, 181–82.

29. Cf. *The Demographic Factors in the Evolution of Nations* (*I fattori demografici dell'evoluzione delle nazioni*), pp. 46–47, 54–61; *The Amount and Composition of the Wealth of the Nations* (*L'ammontare e la composizione della ricchezza delle nazioni*), pp. 429–30.

30. Cf. "Theories upon the Causes of War" ("Teorie sulle cause della guerra"), in *Sociological Problems of War* (*Problemi sociologici della guerra*), pp. 92–93.

II. THE DEATH OF NATIONS

When we speak of the death of a nation, we mean that either its entire population has been extinguished or that it has been so reduced as to render reproduction impossible, as would be the case, for instance, were all the members of one sex to have perished. The death of a nation is clearly a different thing from the dissolution of a state, the structure of which may be shattered either by being broken up into a number of separate political units or by aggregation or submission to another political unit, without its population being injured, much less extinguished thereby.

The deaths of nations, as of individuals, may in the first place be classified into violent and natural deaths. The death of individuals by accident, homicide, or suicide has its counterpart in the extinction of nations as the result of cataclysms, war, or suicide. History records examples of volcanic eruptions and of the submersion of islands whereby whole populations have been wiped out. A legend to which even some scientists give credit tells of the submersion of an entire continent, Atlantis. In any case, instances of this kind are very rare. The death of a nation by suicide is also an extremely rare occurrence; instances of the kind may be said, however, to have occurred when the last remains of a fighting people have preferred death to surrender.

There have certainly been instances of the extinction of whole populations by war, especially in primitive times and among savage tribes, instances in which the conquerors have killed all their vanquished foes or, more frequently, all the males, or in which the latter have been driven into slavery and separated forever from their womenfolk with whom they might have continued to propagate their race. Much more frequently, however, war has not of itself extirpated or does not extirpate a population, although it may have contributed thereto in the case of demographically weak populations. Vigorous populations, on the contrary, recover rapidly from war losses. The effects of wars on nations may be compared to those of wounds on individuals: they heal rapidly in the case of healthy organisms, but feebler ones are likely to succumb.

The death of nations from natural causes is a phenomenon of far greater moment. History records some outstanding instances, such as the disappearance of the original inhabitants of Rome and of many of the ancient Grecian cities.

Examples of the progressive decadence of primitive populations, apparently doomed to certain death, are very numerous. They are to be met with in all continents: in the northern regions of Asia, of Europe, and America, the Australian continent, and the Malayan and Oceanian archipelagoes, the islands off the coast of Indo-China, and the interior of the peninsula, a place in Palestine, central Africa, some of the Indian reservations of Canada and the United States, the virgin forests of the Amazons, and in the extreme South of the American continent.

Two opposite theories are advanced to explain such decadence: one would account for it by the progressive degeneration of the race due to internal biological factors; the other attributes it to external factors: lack of the means of subsistence, abuse of alcoholic drinks, diseases imported by the white people to which the race could offer no resistance.

The problem, however, does not seem to be correctly stated. It is as though we had to decide whether a man dies from natural exhaustion or as the result of disease, vice, or hunger. As a matter of fact, it is rare, indeed, that death cannot be traced to some specific cause and can only be accounted for by the exhaustion of vital force. "Senile decay" is still given as one of the causes of death, although recently the commission appointed to revise the international nomenclature of disease was doubtful as to the desirability of retaining it (1). But death from senility is certainly not a normal phenomenon, and if the term appears frequently in certain statistics this is mainly due to the fact that whenever the precise cause of the death of aged persons is unknown, they are usually classified under this heading (2).

On the other hand, it is certain that numbers of lives are cut short in their prime by diverse diseases, less frequently by vices, and still more rarely because of lack of nourishment.

It is equally certain that a great number of deaths—from one-third to one-half of the total according to the country considered—are due to the concurrence of internal and external factors (3). The organism, having lost with age the vigor of its earlier years, is unable to react against the external causes which undermine its life. In such cases, the so-called "causes of death" might more properly be termed "forms of death," the primary cause being, in fact, the diminution of vital resistance.

It may reasonably be assumed that something analogous to this occurs in respect of populations. These also, as we have shown in the *Introduction* (4), have their vital cycle; and it is natural that, as the end of the cycle approaches, they are often unable to resist the counteraction of external factors. It is somewhat arbitrary to affirm either that these external factors cause the death of nations, and that diminished biological resistance only furnishes favorable conditions for their action, or that diminished biological resistance is the primary cause of their death, while the influence of external factors is only the occasional cause.

This interpretation helps to explain how the same causes to which the disappearance of many primitive populations are attributed—alcoholic abuses, the contagion of tuberculosis, venereal disease, measles, and smallpox, the violent change from ancient forms of social organization to forms to which the race is unaccustomed—have in fact been endured by other races without arresting the rhythm of their growth. The fact is that the former races were decadent and the latter still vigorous.

This same interpretation would likewise account for the fact that certain races which were on the net decrease—the Maoris and Esquimaux, for example—have been able, thanks to timely measures on the part of the European authorities, not only to halt on the downward path but actually to increase in numbers, at least in some localities (5). The fact that an organism is old and destined to decay under certain conditions does not preclude the possibility of its recovering its strength and even prolonging its existence for many years owing to more solicitous and rational care.

Thus we can account also for the gradual extinction of certain races—the pygmies of equatorial Africa may be cited—notwithstanding that they have continuously avoided contact with other populations and are not short of the means of subsistence (6). This is, in fact, an instance of death from senile decay, a phenomenon as rare in races as in individuals.

It would, lastly, account for the fact that, sometimes, when a part of these primitive populations has come into touch and mixed with white men, while another part has kept itself more or less rigorously isolated, the latter has been the first to decline despite the fact that the former should have been the one to suffer from the ill effects of contact with civilization. This has been noted in the case of the Esquimaux in Greenland (7). The fact is that in these instances mixture with the white race has caused an influx of younger and healthier blood, which has arrested the decay of the race, amply compensating for the ill effects of contagion and the relinquishment of primitive customs.

Neither should it be a matter for surprise, after what has been shown in the course of the *Introduc-*

tion, that the nations also die out by natural process. All that lives is doomed to death. Rather is it surprising that such instances of death are rare. But this, too, is explicable.

It is due to two causes. One is the same cause that is responsible for the fact that explorers find no old persons among certain savage tribes. As soon as members of these tribes grow old, they are killed off as being a useless burden on society, and sometimes eaten with a view to the survivors thus acquiring their qualities. Now, until recent times, the more vigorous nations treated those nations that were declining in the same manner as the younger members of these savage tribes treat their elders. As soon as a nation declined in strength, its neighbors fell on it and destroyed or assimilated it, thus cutting short the completion of its cycle of life. Only of recent times has any care been taken of senescent races and an effort made to retard rather than hasten their death. This is true of the Danes in relation to the Esquimaux in Greenland, the English to the aborigines of Australia and the Maoris in New Zealand, as also of the United States and Canada in their treatment of the Red Indians.

Another cause is to be sought in that regulating mechanism provided by nature which tends to favor the permeation by younger populations of those that are ageing, the latter being gradually and without conflict replaced by the former, just as happens in daily life, where the old generation slowly makes room for the younger, and the latter are able progressively and without opposition to develop along their own lines (8).

Among the phases of social metabolism which I have summarily described in my previous lectures, and the stages in the evolution of nations arising therefrom, two phases are definitely to be distinguished: these may be termed respectively the "normal" and the "abnormal." The normal phase is characterized by the fact that the upward social current suffices to restore the upper classes without impoverishing the lower classes whence it originates; this is no longer the case in the abnormal phase, so that the nation suffers from a deficiency of the lower elements of the population.

Let us assume that a population which is still at the first stage comes into contact with a people that has entered on the second one. The poorer and more prolific members of the former, overcoming their attachment to their native land and, not infrequently, a dislike of their neighbor, will seek to better their lot by emigrating and offering their services to the older and richer people, who stand in need of labor. It rarely happens among civilized peoples that such service is at first rejected; where the difference between the two peoples is more pronounced, the offer—albeit somewhat reluctantly made—is the more readily accepted. Thus the younger and more prolific population, often even favored by the older and less prolific one into which it penetrates, invades its lower strata. Where no artificial obstacles are interposed, it gradually rises in the social scale; and, sooner or later, more or less slowly but surely, it penetrates the class above the lowest and, little by little, the middle and upper classes: in this manner it ends by substituting itself for the original stock throughout the whole social organism (9).

History continues to refer to the population of a given locality and of a given name as if it were the same, whereas, as a matter of fact, it has undergone a complete racial change. Unperceived, the old nation has died and a new one has taken its place.

This mechanism of renewal is of paramount importance, since the transmission of civilization is based on it. If each of the several nations were to live boxed up by itself, those which first reached the apex of their development would decline and disappear without being able to hand on to their younger sister-nations the inheritance of their science and civilization. A lengthy education and slow apprenticeship and—condition *sine qua non* to both of these—an adequate process of assimilation, are essential to enable the members of a less-advanced civilization to grasp the fruits of a fully developed one and to take full advantage of them according to their lights. This is precisely what the mechanism to which we have referred provides for, since the immigrant members of the younger nations who work their way into the lower strata of the more evolved ones are assimilated by the new civilization, and all the more readily as, their native culture being low, they are less strongly attached to their own civilization. Such assimilation is, however, scarcely ever complete: the immigrants bring in, together with the fresh blood they contribute, their own sentiments, often some national tradition, sometimes even their own language. The civilization thus produced, while preserving the conquests of the older one, contains also new germs which may develop along new and original lines.

But here again it happens that man not infrequently frustrates the subtle plan of nature. These processes of permeation and substitution of older by younger races, while they usually go on unhindered by artificial barriers in the case of two contiguous races inclosed within the boundaries of one and the same state, are not infrequently checked by an increasing psychological resistance, which is fostered by the authorities, where political barriers divide the two races. Political distrust, economic rivalry, sometimes military reasons, create or embitter a dislike of the foreigners, so that their penetration, which was welcomed and encouraged in the first instance, comes, in the long run, to be hindered in a multitude of ways and under a diversity of pretexts.

Thus, individuals belonging to the different countries no longer spread over the earth like the molecules of a liquid flowing through a series of freely intercommunicating receptacles, but as those of a liquid contained in a series of receptacles separated one from the other by more or less permeable sections which, while not absolutely preventing all forms of osmosis, do produce a considerable diversity of pressure as between the several receptacles. Beyond a certain point the dividing section cannot withstand the pressure, and the liquid pours from the receptacle at higher pressure into that at lower pressure. Beyond a certain point, political barriers break down under demographic pressure and the superabundant population of the younger nation invades, in war, the confines of the older nation.

Thus that process of transfusion of blood from the younger to the older races which might go on peacefully and gradually by natural means, is effected by violent means, giving rise to a discontinuity which cannot but be hurtful to the evolution of civilization.

We may say that it is resistance to the natural process that renders manifest the death of nations. But, fortunately, nature's mechanism generally works sufficiently well to insure that death shall not take place before the nation destined to succumb has transmitted the fruits of its civilization to the survivor. The more pronounced the anthropological diversity and social dissimilarity between the younger, rising nation and the older nation on the downgrade in the parabola of evolution, the less likely is it that the process of permeation will have time to run its full course; and therefore the deeper and more lasting will be the discontinuity in the evolution of civilization. The resistance first of the Greeks and later of the Romans to admitting into their midst the barbarian populations who were so vastly beneath them in culture, made it impossible for the latter to replace the ancient stock without a shock that annihilated the progress of many centuries and caused between the ancient and the modern world the great gap of the Dark Ages.

In any case, if civilization could, and did, revive and flourish once again, this is due to the fact that the barbarian stock, which permeated and was more or less assimilated by the Roman, had gathered and preserved the seed of civilization, destined to fructify again, in a different form, when the conditions necessary to its development arose (10).

But an urgent question arises: What is the present stage of evolution of the peoples of the white race? For, it may be said, this theoretical conception of cycles of the nations is interesting and attractive, but until the future has allowed us to determine to what extent it applies to our conditions we must not lose sight of facts as they are; and these show us that, whatever may be their future fate, at the present day the peoples belonging to the white race continue in all countries to have a more or less notable, but generally a very notable, excess of births over deaths. Before the war this excess amounted each year to 1 per cent of the population, which would have doubled the population in a period of seventy years (11). And if it is true that this rate has now declined in many countries, it cannot on the whole be much below that figure. During the period 1909–23, notwithstanding the losses caused by the war and the influenza epidemic, the coefficient of increase was indeed estimated at between 6 and 7 per 1,000, at which rate the population would double in a little over a century (12).

It is hardly necessary for me to explain to you the fallacy of such an argument after the works of Dublin and Lotka and of Kuczynski (13). They have clearly shown that the excess of births over deaths does not afford an index for forecasting the future growth of populations. The fact is that today the peoples of the white race, at least those of Europe and the United States, are in an unusually advantageous position due to the favorable composition of their age-groups, which, however, can only be transitory. The annual number of births went on increasing until the beginning of this century and then declined. This brings it about that the classes of the central age-groups, which are almost the only ones contributing to the birth-rate and who are not greatly exposed to death, are particularly numerous as compared to the older classes arising from previous and smaller numbers of births, and they are also numerous as compared to the younger classes coming from the already reduced number of births of the ensuing period. This consideration is of capital importance, and I therefore hope I shall be excused if I avail myself of this opportunity to remind you that as far back as 1911, in my lecture on *The Demographic Factors in the Evolution of Nations* (14), I called attention to the importance of the favorable composition of age-groups, which reacts not only on the growth of the population but also on its economic productivity, at a certain stage in the evolution of nations; and at the same time I pointed out that these conditions will inevitably be reversed later on when adults have become old and their place has been taken by the adolescents and children (15).

I also called attention to the fact that this favorable composition of the populations made it difficult to realize the coming crisis, and even gave rise in the nations to a sort of massive optimism at the very time when they were on the eve of decline. I quoted the example of Rome which was glorified as an "Eternal City." Cicero wrote as a great concession. "Let us suppose that Rome lasts another 10,000 years"—and yet Rome, only a few centuries later, had disappeared from the list of states (16).

But if at that time the illusion was excusable, this is no longer the case after the eloquent proofs afforded us by statistics. Dr. Kuczynski shows us that on the supposition that the birth- and death-rates continue to be what they now are, 1,000 women born in 1927 will give birth to only 910 daughters in France, only 830 in Germany, and only 820 in England. The conditions grow worse from year to year. The estimate for the women born in 1926 would give 937 daughters for France, 890 for Germany, and 880 for England. Sweden also already shows a deficit for births of 1926: 1,000 girls born in that year would have given birth to only 950 daughters. Denmark and Finland would still have an excess, with 1,010 daughters per 1,000 girls born in 1926; but the comparison of this figure with those of the previous years shows a steady reduction and makes us think that for those countries also a deficit is imminent, if indeed it has not already begun.

Taken as a whole, the aforesaid countries of Northern and Western Europe in 1926 had a death-rate and a birth-rate under which 100 girls born in that year would be replaced by only 93 girls in the future (17).

In the case of some countries—Germany, the United Kingdom, and France—other authors, by following similar methods, have tried to forecast the date at which the population will reach its maximum. They show that a decline is at our gates: it is due in 1946 in Germany, in 1942 in the United Kingdom, in 1937 in France (18).

Similar calculations have not been made for

other countries, and for many, indeed, the necessary data are lacking; moreover, it is right to say
that it would not be prudent to swear by the results
obtained even for the countries just mentioned.
But a rougher estimate can be made for a still
greater number of countries. Take the number of
persons shown by the latest census returns to be
between the ages of twenty and thirty, and compare it to the average annual number of births during the last years for which data are available. If
we divide the first number by the second multiplied
by 10, we get the percentage of survivors there
should be from present births in order to secure in
twenty or thirty years' time numbers equal to
those returned by the last census. Comparing these
coefficients of survival with those of the life-tables
of their respective countries, we can see where the
population is already virtually on the road to decline. As the number of males between twenty and
thirty years of age recorded in the last census returns in general for 1920 or 1921 was greatly affected by the war, the calculation has been made,
wherever possible, for females. The conclusion to
be drawn is that the population must be considered
as practically declining in England and Wales, in
Scotland (probably also in Ireland), in Finland,
Esthonia, Latvia, Sweden, Norway, France, Belgi-

um, Germany, Switzerland, Austria (and probably also in Hungary (19). The populations of all the states of Western, Northern, and Central Europe must therefore be considered as virtually on the decline, with the sole exceptions of Holland and Denmark.

It has not been possible to make a similar calculation for the whole of the United States, but only for the eleven original registration states (that is, the six states of New England plus the states of New York, New Jersey, Indiana, Michigan, and the District of Columbia). Eight hundred and thirty-four out of 1,000 females born alive in 1926 should survive at the ages between twenty and thirty in order to reproduce the number of females existing in these states according to the census of 1920 (20). Now the life-table for females prepared for 1919–20 gives an average survival-rate about the same, that is, 836 per 1,000 (21); and the small difference perhaps would disappear (if indeed it does not give rise to a difference in the contrary sense) should it be possible to establish the comparisons on the survival-rate of the whole population and not only on that of the white population (22). Only a possible decline of mortality, stronger than the increase of population between twenty and thirty years, from 1919–20 up to the present, may change the conclusion that in these states the population is virtually stationary (23). But it is certain, in any case, for the said states (and the conclusion may likely be extended to others of the present registration area) that the margin is very narrow and that a further decline in the number of births will mean a virtually declining population. It is hardly necessary to add that the general past tendency, as well as the reduced immigration from the most prolific countries, renders that further decline more than probable (24).

The latent population crisis, it is well known, depends on the decline in the birth-rate which has been apparent for more than fifty years past, and this in my opinion has in all probability its roots in biological factors. Many symptoms suggested this. Today we are in the presence of figures which it is difficult to interpret otherwise.

For several countries and towns it is now possible to follow for a series of years the number of first-births classified according to the interval elapsed since marriage. Compare the number of first-children conceived in the first months of marriage with the number of couples—the so-called "unprejudiced marriages"—who, as they had no children in the first nine months, can be considered as having been in a condition to conceive immediately after the nuptials. So we get an index of the nuptial fecundity of the brides, an index which would be satisfactory on the supposition that there were no newly married couples who tried to delay the birth of their first child. It is difficult to assert that this supposition corresponds to the truth; but we may exclude the idea that, for European countries, at least, it is very far removed from it, for as is known, the desire to limit the family is more generally felt after the marriage has given one or more children (25). Statistics of Neo-Malthusian clinics confirm the exceptional nature of cases, in which advice has been given by the clinic to newly married couples desirous of avoiding children. These cases represent only a little over 1 per cent of those to whom consultation has been given (26). In any case, the variation in fecundity shown by these index numbers are so striking that, as we shall see, we must exclude the possibility of explaining them only by the tendency of newly married couples to postpone the birth of their first child.

The frequency with which unprejudiced marriages, or rather those considered as such, give rise to conception within the first three months of conjugal life can be deduced with sufficient approximation to truth from the frequency with which the first child is born within the tenth, eleventh, or twelfth month of the marriage. Now this frequency declines in a striking manner, falling from 38 to 23 per cent in New South Wales from 1893 to 1927; from 39 to 23 per cent in Western Australia from 1900–1902 to 1926–28; from 32 to 25 per cent in the Commonwealth as a whole from 1909 to 1926–27; from 28 to 20 per cent in New Zealand from 1914 to 1927; from 26 to 21 per cent in Dresden from 1891–94 to 1905–8; from 19 to 6.6 per cent in Chemnitz from 1911 to 1926–28; from 16 to 6.4 per cent for the whole of the former Kingdom of Saxony from 1911 to 1927; from 27 to 14 per cent in Amsterdam from 1910 to 1928; from 15 to less than 10 per cent in Zurich from 1914 to 1927–28 (27).

In almost all cases there has been a decline of over one-third, often of one-half, and in some cases even of two-thirds in the level of fecundity as compared to that at the beginning of the period considered, which, moreover, does not date back very far.

The smaller number of conceptions recorded in the first months are compensated to some extent by those occurring later on (28). The decline is thus to some extent merely in the nature of a delay in the conception of the first child, but only to some extent. Indeed, in many countries a comparison between the number of first-children born after nine months of marriages and the number of un-prejudiced marriages clearly shows that the number of childless marriages has considerably increased (29).

In New South Wales the first-births recorded in 1893 represented 74 per cent of the marriages celebrated in that year; and those recorded in 1927, 58 per cent. In Western Australia they represented, in 1902, 87 per cent; and in 1926–28, 65 per cent. For the Commonwealth as a whole the percentage of marriages followed by first-births within the year passed from 66 in 1909 to 61 in 1926–27; in New Zealand from 69 per cent in 1914 to less than 60 per cent in 1927; in the former Kingdom of Saxony from 38 per cent in 1911–12 to 33 per cent in 1927; in Chemnitz from 44 per cent in 1911–12 to 37 per cent in 1927–28; in Amsterdam from 57 per cent in 1910–11 to 52 per cent in 1925–28.

The conclusion is that not only has conception in the first months of marriage been less frequent but, on the whole, the percentage of childless marriages has increased. It should be noted that the greater length of life, by prolonging the duration of marriages, should have led to quite opposite results. Nor can the phenomenon be explained by the frequency of marriages following prenuptial conception, as, on the contrary, at least the number of prenuptial conceptions followed by births after marriage has declined rather than increased during the period and in the countries under consideration (30), thus affording another reason why we might have expected that the percentage of unprejudiced marriages not followed by a birth after the first nine months would have declined rather than increased.

Moreover, the reductions noted in the percentages of unprejudiced marriages followed by conception within the first three months cannot well be explained only by the growing spread of contraceptive practices. Even if we would admit, for instance, that in Chemnitz, and in the former Kingdom of Saxony as a whole, contraceptive practices were not resorted to in 1911 by newly-married couples, we should have to admit that in recent years nearly two-thirds of the newly wedded couples not only resorted to them but succeeded in their object of avoiding fertilization during the first three months after marriage. The hypothesis, in itself unlikely, seems altogether inadmissible when we reflect that the result of contraceptive practices is very uncertain, so that it is doubtful whether, on an average, they secure the desired results in two-thirds of the cases in point

(31). This means that, even if all the married couples had had recourse to contraceptive practices in 1926–28 and none in 1911, it would not even then be possible to account by this cause for the decline in conceptions during the first three months of marriage to the extent to which it has occurred at Chemnitz or in Saxony as a whole. But when we bear in mind what the practical frequency of contraceptive practices on the part of new couples is likely to be (32), it becomes evident that the reduction in the percentage which has occurred also in other countries, and which amounts to half or one-third of the former level, is very hard to account for by this factor alone.

No statistics bearing on this subject have been published for France—a country which is of special interest from this point of view—but the Direction of French General Statistics has very kindly abstracted for my special benefit the data on first-births in 1925 in the notably prolific department of the Côtes du Nord, and in those of the Haute Garonne and of Gers, in which, on the contrary, the birth-rate has been declining for a long time past. The results are particularly instructive. The frequency with which marriages, considered as unprejudiced, are followed by conception within the first three months of married life amounts to 25

per cent for the Côtes du Nord, and to only 13 and
10 per cent respectively for the Haute Garonne
and the Gers. The same line of argument set forth
above shows that here again these differences cannot be accounted for exclusively by the difference
in the spread of contraceptive practices.

A thorough study is being made in Italy, at my
suggestion, of all the data referring to first-children
born in 1927. The data, although not yet final,
(33), are most suggestive. The percentages of the
marriages considered as unprejudiced, in which the
first child was conceived during the first three
months, have been calculated, not only for all the
regions but also separately for the municipalities,
which, as they have a center of population of more
than 10,000 inhabitants, can be considered as urban, and for the other municipalities considered as
rural. Now the percentages are not regularly higher for the rural districts: this happens in about half
of the cases (and precisely for ten of the eighteen
regions), and the differences are distributed in such
a manner as not to appear systematical. This leads
one to think that the percentages are not greatly
influenced by contraceptive practices. In fact, it
is clear that, if contraceptive practices had a per-
ceptible influence on the number of conceptions
within the first months of marriage, the percentage

of conceptions should be lower in big centers, where such practices are certainly more general. This admitted, the comparison between the percentages of conceptions during the first three months of marriage and the birth-rate assumes special interest. There exists between these percentages and the birth-rate a close correlation, the coefficient of correlation, according to the formula of Bravais, being $+0.70$. This result is quite important, as it means that the differences which occur between the birth-rates of the various Italian regions depend largely on the differences in nuptial fertility of the population (34).

The data set forth above, referring to ten countries or cities, confirm the belief that the decline in the birth-rate is serious, more especially among the populations of Northern, Central, and Western Europe. As we have seen, while the percentage of conceptions in the first three months of married life never falls below 20 per cent in Italy, and also in Australia, notwithstanding the notable decline shown by the figures for the latter country, on the contrary in the different German localities for which recent data are available (for Dresden they cease in 1908), as well as in the towns of Amsterdam and Zurich and in the two French departments of the Haute Garonne and the Gers, which are suffering from a severe decline in the birth-rate, the percentage has fallen below 15 per cent and even falls sometimes as low as 6.5 per cent.

What are the consequences of such a situation? It is evident that, if the tendency above described were to persist, the populations of Northern, Central, and Western Europe would, if isolated, die out in the course of time; but if no political barriers or psychological disinclinations were to hinder the free circulation of natives and foreigners, immigration would provide for the leveling out of the differences in the pressure of population as between those countries and their neighboring peoples.

Realities stand between these two extremes. Until now a notable current of immigration has only been directed toward France, where, more especially since the war, the insufficiency of population is keenly felt. In the period intervening between the census of 1921 and that of 1926 the excess of immigration over emigration has averaged 220,000 persons a year. By adding to this number the natural increase which approximates 80,000, a total annual increase of over 300,000 inhabitants is obtained (35). The figure is undoubtedly a large one, but it is relatively lower than that for the other Latin peoples, not to speak of the outer circle of the Slav populations. Thus the disparity in the pressure of population in France and these other nations, instead of declining, seems, at least for the present, to be increasing. Moreover, a certain degree of resistance to further immigration may already be observed in the psychology of the French; the policy of forced assimilation of foreigners is a clear sign of this; it will probably have the result of checking the current of immigration. In England, where the impression that the country is over-populated is still very common, far from facilitating immigration, they have taken notable steps since the war to limit it.

Will the countries of Northern, Central, and Western Europe throw their doors open in due time to the immigration of the less senescent populations which surround them, and thus share in their demographic evolution? Or will the disparity in the pressure of population go on increasing until it gives rise to a new and yet more tremendous cyclone which will drive the peoples of Eastern and Southern Europe into countries where the pressure of population is less intense? This is a grave query.

Another query arises as to whether the birth-rate in Northern, Central, and Western Europe will continue to be essentially different from that in the countries of Southern and Eastern Europe or whether the former have only preceded the latter by a few years (and the same inquiry might be made for pure populations of the European race in other continents) on the road of a declining birthrate. If the latter alternative is the correct one, then, in a more or less remote future, the disparity will inevitably arise no longer between the several populations of the European race but between European races on the one hand and the Hindu, Malayan, and yellow races on the other.

The two queries throw their shadow threateningly across the future of civilization. At the present time science does not possess the requisite data for giving a reply.

NOTES

1. I refer to the discussions which took place at the "Commission mixte" (Institut International de Statistique et Organisation d'Hygiène de la S.d.N.), chargée par le gouvernement français de coordonner les réponses des gouvernements au sujet de la quatrième révision de la nomenclature des causes des décès, at the meeting in Paris from April 9–12, 1929.

2. It has been brought to light, for instance, for cancer, in the studies upon the frequency of that cause of death made by the Health Organisation of the League of Nations. It seems evident that a larger or smaller number, according to the countries, of deaths from cancer are returned as deaths from senility. Cf. *Rapport sur les travaux de la Commission du Cancer de 1923 à 1927*, November 1, 1927, League of Nations, Health Organisation C.H. 631 (1) (C. H. Cancer) 42 (2), p. 9; and *Considérations sur les rapports présumés entre le cancer et la race d'après l'étude des statistiques anthropologiques et mé-*

dicales de quelques pays d'Europe, by M. Alfredo Niceforo and Eugène Pittard Genève, 1926), League of Nations, Health Organisation, Commission on Cancer C. H. 492.

3. It is known that Lexis has tried to isolate a normal group of deaths, having its center, according to the countries, at seventy to eighty years of age, from precocious deaths during infancy, youth, or adult age. These deaths at a normal age, with few exceptions, for deaths from senility, are precisely those which can be attributed to the joint action of interior and exterior factors. According to Benini's data, this normal group represents a percentage of total deaths varying from 32 per cent in Spain to over 49 per cent in Japan (R. Benini, *The Principles of Demography* [*Principii di demografia*] [Florence: Barbera, 1901]).

4. Cf. pp. 3–12.

5. We must, however, take into consideration the disturbing influences exercised on the comparisons by (*a*) the varying accuracy of the successive census (cf. "The Laws of the Evolution of Population" ["Le leggi di evoluzione della popolazione"], p. 275); (*b*) and the different proportion of hybrids (cf., on this point, the following lecture, *The Birth and Revival of Nations*, p. 110, and especially the note 36).

6. The pigmies of whom Herodotus and Pliny have given us information are living, and more have been living, in such complete isolation in virgin forests or deserted planes or in rocky countries that for many centuries their existence has been doubted; while they, for their part, ignored the existence of a part of the globe populated with white people (cf. A. Marazzi, *Between the Savages and the Civilized People* ["*Fra i selvaggi e fra i civilizzati*"] [Milano: Istituto Editoriale Scientifico], pp. 113–40). They know they once occupied a far larger territory and that, on the arrival of taller and stronger people, they withdrew back without fighting (*ibid.*, 139). Even where they live in zones near the ones occupied by other races, they live completely apart. As regards the Batua, the Duchess of Aosta informs us that they are so savage that they hide themselves not only from the white people but also from other Negroes, whom they do not call by the

name of "man," and for nothing in the world would they eat with them or enter into huts (Elena di Francia, Duchessa d'Aosta, *Travels in Africa* [*Viaggi in Africa*] [Milano: Treves, 1913], p. 265).

7. Cf., on this point, particularly by Carega, "Alcuni dati demografici sugli Esquimesi," *Metron*, VI (1928), 30.

8. Cf. "Latent Factors of War" ("Fattori latenti delle guerre"), in *Sociological Problems of War* (*Problemi sociologici della guerra*), pp. 15–17; "The Laws of the Evolution of Populations" ("Le leggi di evoluzione della popolazione"), pp. 292–93; "Population Movements" ("Les mouvements de population"), pp. 813–14.

9. Cf. the articles cited in the preceding note and "The Different Growth of Social Classes" ("Il diverso accrescimento delle classi sociali"), pp. 64–66.

10. Cf., on the foregoing, particularly: "Latent Factors of War" ("Fattori latenti della guerre"), pp. 17–19; "The Laws of the Evolution of Populations" ("Le leggi di evoluzione della popolazione"), pp. 293–95; "Population Movements" ("Les mouvements de population"), pp. 812–14.

11. Cf. the "Introduction" to "The Dynamics of Populations" ("La dinamica delle popolazioni"), in *Treatise on Hygiene* (*Trattato di igiene*), directed by Professor O. Casagrandi (Torino: Utet, 1929).

12. Cf. C. H. Knibbs, *The Shadow of the World's Future*, quoted, p. 49, n.

13. L. I. Dublin and A. J. Lotka, "On the True Rate of Natural Increase," *Journal of the American Statistical Association*, September, 1925; L. I. Dublin, "The Statistician and the Population Problem, *Population Problems in the United States and Canada* (Boston: Houghton Mifflin Co., 1926); A. J. Lotka, "The Progressive Adjustment of Age Distribution to Fecundity," *Journal of the Washington Academy of Sciences*, November 18, 1926; R. R. Kuczynski, *The Balance of Births and Deaths*, Vol. I, *Western and Northern Europe* (New York: Macmillan Co., 1928).

14. The lecture was given in Trieste in April, 1911. A summary was published the same year in the "Rivista italiana di Sociologia."

THE DEATH OF NATIONS

The following year the lecture was printed by F.lli Bocca (Turin) in a volume containing in its notes an extensive documentation.

15. Cf. pp. 37, 38, 40, 41, 63, 70, 71, 72, of the said volume.

16. Cf. pp. 37 and 40 of the said volume.

17. See the chapter "Net Reproduction Rates" of Kuczynski's work, particularly pp. 52–54.

18. See, for France, Alfred Sauvy, "La population française jusqu'au 1956. Essai de prévision démographique," *Journal de la Société de Statistique de Paris*, December, 1928, and January, 1929, pp. 325–26; for the United Kingdom, A. L. Bowley "Births and Population in Great Britain," *Economic Journal*, June, 1924, p. 189; for Germany, "Richtlinien zur Beurteilung des Bevölkerungsproblems Deutschlands für die naechsten 50 Jahren." *Statistik des deutschen Reiches*, CCCXVI, pp. 39, 42.

These forecasts are analyzed and discussed in the study above quoted on the *Dynamics of Populations* (*Dinamica delle popolazioni*).

19. In the following table, Part A contains the data for states whose population is virtually declining; Part B, the data for states whose population appears to increase. We cannot avail ourselves, for all the states, of life-tables from which it is possible to calculate the average number of survivals at twenty to thirty years; but the conclusion is often equally clear. This is the case in the first place when the ratio at column 6 is higher than the unit, which means that even if none of the women born died before thirty years of age, it would not be possible to reproduce the number of women returned by the last census from the women born during the last years. This is the case for Austria, Esthonia, Germany, England, Sweden, and Switzerland. At other times the conclusion is justified by comparisons with the data deducted from mortality tables for states where economic and demographic conditions are similar. Thus it is difficult to admit that the average survival in Scotland is higher than 0.881, when this percentage is only exceeded in New Zealand and Australia, and when in England the corresponding figure is 0.847. It should be noted that for India the effective survival-rate (0.413) is lower than that (0.509) re-

| | | | FEMALES BORN | | AVERAGE SURVIVAL RATE | | |
| | | | | | | At 20–30 Years According to the Last Life-Table | |
STATES	DATE OF LAST CENSUS	LIVING WOMEN 20–30 YEARS OF AGE AT LAST CENSUS	During Years	Yearly Average	Necessary to Maintain Constant the Female Population	Years	Actual Survival-Rate
(1)	(2)	(3)	(4)	(5)	(6)	(7)	(8)
			Part A				
Austria........	1923	600,514 (calculated)	1927–28*	57,073	1.052		
Belgium.......	1920	653,244	1927–28	71,047	0.919		
Esthonia......	1922	98,793	1927–28	9,530	1.036		
France†.......	1921	3,190,587	1927–28	363,197	0.878	1920–23	0.813
Finland.......	1920	277,604	1926–27	37,016	0.749	1911–20	0.727
Germany‡(3)..	1925	5,925,149	1927–28	568,486	1.042	1924–26	0.844
England and Wales.......	1921	3,323,357	1927–28	321,959	1.032	1920–22	0.847
Ireland§......	1911	356,121	1921–23	44,425	0.801		
Latvia.......	1925	174,078	1926–27	20,005	0.870		
Norway.......	1920	218,253	1927–28	24,579	0.887	1911–21	0.835
Scotland......	1921	429,727	1926–27	48,723	0.881		
Sweden.......	1922	494,043	1927–28	47,666	1.036	1916–20	0.818
Switzerland....	1920	345,816	1927–28	33,788	1.023	1920–21	0.847
Hungary......	1920	745,962	1927–28	105,937	0.704	1900–1905	0.582
			Part B				
Italy.........	1921	3,264,522	1927–28	526,313	0.620	1921–22	0.739
Spain.........	1920	1,775,928	1927–28	313,152	0.567		
Roumania‖ ...	1927	1,340,052 (calculated)	1926–27	293,497	0.456	....	0.640
Bulgaria......	1920	399,535	1926–27	75,974	0.526	1900–05	0.623
Denmark......	1921	278,149	1927–28	33,211	0.838	1921–25	0.874
Czechoslovakia	1921	1,249,273	1926–27	166,230	0.752		
Netherlands...	1920	572,421	1927–28	85,535	0.669	1910–20	0.820
U.R.S.S. (Europe)¶...	1926	10,231,790	1926–27	2,141,722	0.478		
Argentine.....	1914	705,804	1925–26	144,325	0.489	1914	0.715
Chile.........	1920	344,463	1926–27	80,190	0.430		
Canada......	1921	699,101	1926–27	113,210	0.618		
Japan**.......	1925	4,622,697	1926–27	1,017,201	0.454	1908–13	0.673
British India††	1921	20,699,270	1926–27	4,070,115	0.509	1901–11	0.413
Egypt‡‡......	1927	1,156,131 (calculated)	1926–27	299,264	0.386		
Union South Africa§§....	1926	137,170	1927–28	21,633	0.634	1920–22	0.847
Australia......	1921	468,674	1927–28	64,908	0.722	1921–22	0.887
New Zealand ..	1926	106,677	1927–28	13,414	0.795	1921–22	0.913

[Footnotes to Table on Following Page]

quired to restore the female population; but the life-table from which the actual rate of survival has been calculated is out of date (1910–11). Probably today the survival-rate is considerably higher.

20. The number of females born alive in 1926 amounted to 303,465; that of females of twenty to thirty years of age returned in the census of 1920 was 2,531,420.

21. The average survival-rate for white females from twenty to twenty-nine years of age is 84,467 per 100 for the registration area, 1919–20, being based upon the yearly survival-rate calculated by the Metropolitan Life Insurance Company (American Life Table by Individual Years, *Statistical Bulletin*, August, 1928, p. 8). In the eleven states of the original registration area the survival-rate is somewhat lower for the females of seventeen, twenty-two, twenty-seven and thirty-two years of age; its ratio to the one of the corresponding ages for the registration area, 1919–20, was 98,96 to 100 (cf. for the data, *United States Abridged Life Tables*, 1919–20, prepared by Elbertie Foudray (Washington: Government Printing Office, 1923). The average of the survival-rate for twenty to twenty-nine years in 1919–20 for the original registration area can be placed then at $84,467 \times 0.9896 = 83,592$ per 100.

22. This conclusion is suggested by the result of an approximate calculation of the survival-rate of the whole population. In the eleven

---

* For the years italicized, we know only the total number of births. The subdivision between the sexes has been made proportionally to the last two years with known distribution.

† Comprising also Alsace Lorraine.

‡ Excluding the Saar territory.

§ The whole island.

‖ Triple the class registered in 1899 (in proportion to the increase of the total population in 1927).

¶ Minus the independent republics of Bashkiria and Daghestan and the governorships of Ivanovo-Voznessensk and North Caucasus. For these countries the class 20–30 is calculated at the same ratio as that of the U.S.S.R.

** Japan proper. Population of Japan proper, 59,736,822; of Empire, 83,456,929.

†† The births refer to a part of the population and precisely in 1925 to 241,469,-026; in 1926 to 241,471,383. Thus the total population has been reduced from 315,-850,442 to 241,470,205.

‡‡ Class of survivors of 20–30 years of age calculated on the basis of the total population registered in 1927 according to the age distribution of the census of 1917.

§§ Only Europeans.

original registration states the census of 1920 showed that 97.6 per cent of the population was white and 2.4 per cent colored. Attributing to this the survival-rate calculated for the colored of said states, and weighing the survival-rates of the white and of the colored people (cf. *United States Abridged Life Tables*, 1919–20, above mentioned) according to the percentages above stated, the survival-rate resulting for the total female population for the ages of seventeen, twenty-two, twenty-seven, and thirty-two years stands to that of the white female population as 995.95 to 1,000. By applying this to the survival-rate of 83,592 above arrived at for the white female population of twenty to twenty-nine years of age, we obtain the survival-rate of 83,253 for the total female population.

23. The Metropolitan Life Insurance Company has brought to light that from 1921 to 1927 the average duration of life has not increased except at birth. After the first year, it has declined (cf. "A Setback in Mid-Life Mortality," *Statistical Bulletin*, February, 1929). The yearly survival-rate for the registration area of today, which I have calculated after obtaining the yearly death-rates by interpolation, is somewhat higher up to sixty-two years. The average of the ten survival rates from twenty to twenty-nine years of age is 84,494 in 1921 and 87,775 in 1927.

24. After this lecture Dr. Dublin and Dr. Lotka have kindly, at my request, brought their calculations up to date in an article: "The True Rate of Natural Increase of the Population of the United States, Revision on Basis of Recent Data," which will appear in the next number of *Metron*. They show *inter alia*, that the birth-rate necessary to maintain constant the white population, owing to the age distribution of the females calculated for 1928, is to be placed at 18.4°/oo, for the total of the states included in the registration area of 1920. As a matter of fact, the birth-rate observed was 19.4°/oo. At this point let me quote from the proofs of their article: "The effective fertility of our population is separated by a closer margin from the minimum consistent with undiminished numbers than appears on the surface, and than most of us have probably supposed. The last birth-rate figures

published by the government show a decline of one full unit per thousand, as compared with the immediately preceding year. Should the next year by any chance exhibit a repetition of such a decline by a full point, we should actually have reached a birth-rate of 18.4, practically the same figure that has been shown above to correspond to just that fertility which, with the existing age distribution, will only just suffice to keep the population at standstill. Any further decline in fertility would, in the absence of immigration, mean ultimately a *diminished* population, even though for a time this might not become apparent owing to the residual effects of past higher fertility."

25. See, in this regard, "The Fertility of Woman in Relation to the Problem of Population" ("La fertilità della donna in relazione al problema della popolazione"), *Economia*, August–September, 1927; and "Population Problems" ("Problemi della popolazione"), *Annali dell'Istituto di Statistica* (Bari: Royal University, 1928).

26. The data for the Mother's Clinic of London are often quoted in this connection. They have been published by the Director of the clinic, Dr. Marie Stopes *The First Five Thousand*, The First Report of the First British Birth Control Clinic, p. 20) and then quoted by Dr. M. T. Nisot, *La question eugénique dans les divers pays* ("*The Eugenic Question in Various Countries*") (Brussels: Camponhout, Tome 1er, p. 123).

27. Stillbirths are excluded from these figures, but the data for Amsterdam, for which it was possible to make the calculation taking into account stillbirths also, show that the influence exercised by their inclusion is insignificant, as it only affects the third significant figure.

28. The percentage of all first-children born after nine months of marriage, represented by those born within the tenth, eleventh, and twelfth months, is declining in most states. It has fallen in the intervals above stated, from 45 to 31 per cent in New South Wales; from 38 to 29 per cent in Western Australia; from 40 to 30 per cent in the whole Australian Confederation; from 32 to 28 per cent in New Zealand; from 42 to 36 per cent in Dresden; from 34 to 13 per cent in Chemnitz; from 35 to 15 per cent in the whole of the former Kingdom

of Saxony; from 40 to 22 per cent in Amsterdam; from 31 to 20 per cent in Zurich.

29. Only the two towns of Zurich and Dresden make an exception. For them the decrease of the percentage of the conceptions in the three first months of marriage was not very great; and the period of observation was, on the other hand, rather short.

30. The ratio of first-children born during the first nine months of the marriage to the marriages from which they are presumably derived (weighted average of the marriages of the preceding year (seven-eighths) and of those during the same year (one-eighth) changes in New South Wales from 26 per cent during 1893–95 to 28 per cent during 1923–27; in Western Australia from 23 per cent during 1900–1902 to 24 per cent in 1926–28; for the whole Australian Confederation from 29 per cent in 1909 to 24 per cent in 1926–27; in New Zealand from 24 per cent in 1914 to 23 per cent in 1924–27; in Dresden from 38 per cent during 1891 to 31 per cent in 1908; in Chemnitz from 34 per cent in 1911 to 25 per cent in 1927–28; in the whole of the former Kingdom of Saxony from 33 per cent in 1911 to 23 per cent in 1927; in Amsterdam from 26 per cent in 1910 to 22 per cent in 1928; in Zürich from 22 per cent in 1914 to 16 per cent in 1927–28.

31. See, in this regard, the pamphlet of Dr. Stopes, *The First Five Thousand*, and the volume of Dr. J. Cooper, *The Technique of Contraception* (New York: Day-Nichols, 1928), which agree in giving 83 or 84 per cent of failures for couples having recourse to contraceptive practices before consulting the clinic.

32. In one of the round-tables conferences held at the University of Chicago (Harris Foundation) on population, Mrs. Margaret Sanger, the well-known advocate of birth-control, when questioned on this point, stated that she thought that in England during the last five years it could be said that 60 per cent of the families were acquainted with birth-control means. In a state like New York, she added, the percentage may be lower. Talking during another conference on the same argument, Dr. L. I. Dublin, chief statistician of the Metropolitan Life Insurance Company, declared he considered the percentages

given by Mrs. Sanger exaggerated if referred to the total population and only admissible for the urban populations.

In the above-mentioned investigation by Dr. Hamilton 87 per cent of the 100 married women questioned stated that they had made use of birth-control practices. In another investigation by Dr. Davis, upon 985 married women who returned the questionnaire sent them, 74.11 per cent made the same declaration (K. B. Davis, "A Study of the Sex Life of the Normal Married Woman," *Journal of Social Hygiene*, April, 1922). The persons questioned by Dr. Hamilton and those who replied to the questionnaire of Dr. Davis were very likely not representative of the whole population; those questioned by Dr. Hamilton belonged to the intellectual classes, and those who replied to the questionnaire must have been, as is always the case when sending out questionnaires, selected among the same category; now it is hardly necessary to call attention to the fact that Neo-Malthusian practices are more frequent in the intellectual classes.

It should be kept in mind that the results of Dr. Davis and of Dr. Hamilton, as also those of Mrs. Sanger, refer to the percentage of *all* couples who have made use of birth control in some time of their conjugal life and not to that—evidently far smaller—of the *new* couples who had recourse to contraceptive practices during the three first months of marriage.

33. The data are not yet final, as it is not yet possible to make a classification for some first-children, for whom the interval between the marriage and the birth still remains unknown; classification will be possible only when the inquiry is finished. In the computation of the data of the following table, the supposition has been adopted that the first-born children, for whom the interval had not been indicated, should be distributed, as regards this interval, in the same proportion as other first-children, but it is quite possible that this supposition does not correspond exactly to the facts.

34. The following table gives, in columns 3, 4, and 5, the percentages of conceptions within the first three months of conjugal life (deducted from the percentages of the unprejudiced marriages

which had the first child within the tenth, eleventh, or twelfth month after the nuptials) in urban centers, in rural communes, and in the entire region; whereas in column 1 the birth-rates are indicated. The regions are graduated according to the increasing intensity of the birth-rate, and it is easy to see from the data in column 5 that the

Regions	Birth-Rates in 1926 (per 1,000 Inhabitants) (1)	Percentages of the Marriages Which Had the First Child within the First Nine Months after the Nuptials (2)	Percentages of the Unprejudiced Marriages Which Had the First Child Within the Tenth, Eleventh, and Twelfth Month after the Nuptials		
			Urban Centers (3)	Rural Communes (4)	Total (5)
Liguria..........	17.12	14.81	28.6	26.0	27.5
Piedmont........	17.69	12.19	21.5	22.2	22.0
Tuscany.........	22.19	22.24	30.9	29.2	29.7
Julian Venetia...	22.85	30.42	17.3	26.3	22.5
Tridentine Venetia	25.01	23.34	26.7	34.7	32.9
Emilia..........	25.02	31.71	23.9	21.5	22.2
Lombardy.......	25.10	17.69	27.3	31.0	29.9
Sicily...........	26.75	12.16	30.7	32.9	31.3
The Marches.....	28.01	22.22	33.9	36.7	36.1
Latium..........	28.04	16.33	35.9	32.7	33.9
Umbria.........	28.37	22.21	32.6	30.6	31.1
Venetia.........	29.27	30.66	34.0	27.2	28.3
Sardinia.........	31.72	18.14	27.5	31.2	30.7
Campania.......	32.02	9.87	25.3	33.5	30.7
Abruzzi and Molise	32.09	11.67	33.3	32.5	32.6
Calabria.........	32.50	9.33	35.0	36.0	35.9
Apulia..........	34.04	15.77	35.1	35.7	35.3
Basilicata........	36.62	7.89	41.3	35.4	36.2

percentages of the conceptions during the first three months of married life also show, although with considerable fluctuations, a rising trend. It is probable that the correlation between the figures of columns 1 and 5 would be even higher if the disturbing factor of pre-nuptial conceptions did not interfere; they probably eliminate from these calculations the most prolific portion of the women, the importance of the elimination being greater or lesser as the frequency of said conceptions is higher or lower. If account is taken of pre-nuptial conceptions which give birth to a first child after the nuptials (cf. col.

2), the discrepancies between the figures of columns 1 and 5 are partly explained. The value of the percentages of conceptions within the first three months of marriage, calculated in function of the figures of columns 2 and 3, give, as a matter of fact, better approximations to the values observed and given in column 5 than do the values calculated only in function of the figures of column 1.

35. See the study already quoted upon *The Dynamics of Population* (*La dinamica delle popolazioni*), chapter "France."

III. THE BIRTH AND REVIVAL
OF NATIONS

Two obscure points have for a long time given pause for thought in connection with the theory of the cyclical development of nations, namely, the birth and the revival of nations.

It is clear that if nations describe a cycle, this presupposes a beginning, that is to say, the nation's birth. On the other hand, history records many instances of the revival of nations which, at the first glance, do not fit in easily with the cyclical theory. Many nations have had in their history periods that come to be known as their "rebirth," "renaissance," *"risorgimento"* (rearising), "resurrection," etc. In Italy, in addition to the renaissance and the *risorgimento*, the period of the Communes offers another instance of revival; and—unless we are laboring under a false impression—we have at the present time entered upon a fourth such period. Japan gave a most conspicuous example of the kind during the second half of last century.

I shall endeavor in this lecture to throw some light on these two points. That which concerns the birth of nations, or, to put it more generally, the arising of new races, is undoubtedly one of the most enthralling problems on the agenda of the International Union for the Scientific Investigations on Population Problems, which was set up in Paris following the World Population Conference held in Geneva in 1927. The Italian Committee on Population—one of the most flourishing and promising of the national associations of which the International Union is built up—has the intention of specially setting itself to the study of this problem, organizing for the purpose special expeditions into those countries where new races are believed to be in the course of formation (1).

The rise of new races or nations is apparently to be considered as a phenomenon of crossbreeding. It has, indeed, long been observed that new civilizations and nations frequently result from the mixing or the juxtaposition or superimposition of different populations (2), but this result has been attributed to mutual cultural and political influences rather than to a biological phenomenon (3). Thus the United States of America today, which certainly constitutes a great new nation and—from some points of view—also a new race, is the result of the mixture of individuals belonging to the most diverse races and nations. In like manner, the English nation dates from the conquest of Great Britain by the Normans, who mixed with the previous population, formed of Mediterranean and Nordic elements, and perhaps also of the remains of brachycephalics who had at some period found their way into the island. The origin of the French people is analogous, being due to the superposition of a Germanic stock—after which the country is named—on the preceding population of Alpine, Mediterranean, and Nordic origin. Germany, in like manner, has grown out of the combination of Germanic with Slav and Alpine populations, nor has she possibly lost all trace of the Mediterranean blood brought in by the Roman Conquest. The same races, though in very different proportions, enter into the composition of the Italian population.

According to tradition, which is borne out by a multitude of indications and evidences, the ancient civilizations of Greece, Etruria, and Rome derived their origin from the invasions of new populations who superimposed themselves on the ancient ones of more or less different race.

It is not improbable that, if certain nations have long been supposed by us to consist of a single race, this is due to our lack of knowledge concerning them. Egypt, for instance, which, apart from the later filtering-in of Negroid blood, had been regarded as being of purely Mediterranean race, seems in the light of modern investigation to be the product of a combination—that is to say, of people of a brachycephalic race, described as "Armenoid," superposing themselves on a Mediterranean population (4), without counting the presence, that certain indications point to, of blond dolichocephalic people (5).

This phenomenon of superposition and intermixture has generally been supposed to be beneficial mainly or solely from the standpoint of culture and organization. Owing to the fact that crossbreeding has generally regarded as tending to the deterioration of offspring from the standpoint of both quantity and quality, it was consequently inadmissible that it should form a sound basis for the constitution of a healthy and progressive race. It is, in fact, certain that many half-bloods, more especially the mulattoes, are often regarded as being inferior to both of the races whence they are derived (6). Moreover, the statistics of mixed marriages, which we possess for several countries, point to a less degree of fertility than the average fertility of the population (7).

There was another reason for assuming that crossbreeding could not be a sound basis for producing new races. This was the fact that the great nations do apparently present a very distinctive and uniform type. This is true of the nations which are regarded as most advanced at the present time, and more especially of the English and German. Also, so far as we can judge from tradition and from surviving works of art, it was true of the Egyptians, the Assyrians, the Greeks and the Romans.

The study of the products of crossbreeding which has been carried on methodically for some years past, is, however, beginning to cast some light on this question and to suggest an explanation for these apparent contradictions.

If we consider separately the several characteristics of hybrids, they do not apparently reveal any systematic tendency to degeneration as compared with the parent's characteristics. Heredity can generally be put in accordance with the Mendelian laws; thus, if the offspring may sometimes display unfavorable characteristics which were not visible in the parents, this is because the said characters are frequently recessive (this is generally true of unfavorable characters) and therefore remained latent in the forebears. The unfavorable characteristics of cross-bloods in such cases are not a sign of degeneration but are merely the result of that scission which is typical of the Mendelian laws and which is to be met with also in the offspring of heterozygotic individuals of the same race (8).

Neither is the variability of the several characters always more marked in hybrids than in the parent-races whence they are derived (9).

Passing from the consideration of the several characters to that of their mutual relationship, we find among the cross-breeds that, if the several characters are not transmitted with that complete independence one from the other which the Mendelian laws would lead us to expect, the connection between them is, in any case, but limited.

Thus mixed breeding produces a multiplicity of combinations of characters which, in the great majority of cases, results in offspring who stand half-way, in point of efficiency, between the two original stocks; but it is also apt, with greater or lesser frequency, to produce a superior or inferior combination, when a number of either favorable or unfavorable characters, belonging to the parent-races, are combined in the children (10).

It is only natural that the diverse characters which are thus associated in the organisms of the offspring cannot always blend successfully, notwithstanding the mutual influence exercised during development, and this gives rise to such physical, intellectual, and moral dissonances which are found in hybrids and which strike sometimes even the casual observer in countries where several races intermix (11). It is dissonances such as these that are responsible for the unfavorable view taken of half-bloods, and not without reason, since they must tend to lessen physical resistance in the off-spring, at least during the earliest stage of development, while, so far as mental and moral qualities are concerned, they certainly represent a serious social problem.

Such ill-blended offspring of crossbreeding, as well as the particularly unfavorable combinations which it is apt to produce, can however be rigorously eliminated if the cross-race is subjected to intensive natural selection. Such selection does actually take place, either through the struggle for life resulting from natural obstacles or enemy groups or through sexual selection or through emigration which—as I will have occasion to show later—is no casual phenomenon but one that provides systematically for removing from communities those individuals who are, for the time being, ill adapted to form part thereof and for directing them to the environment best suited to them (12). Emigration thus becomes a powerful means of adaptation, on one side purifying and giving homogeneity to the populations from whom it comes, and on the other, providing other countries with the individuals who are pre-adapted to them.

The struggle for life, sexual selection, and em-igration account for the fact that the most ad-vanced nations, notwithstanding the fact that they owe their origins to the fusion of anthropologically heterogeneous elements and that they must prob-ably in their beginnings have presented very con-siderable and marked diversity of forms, grow more and more homogeneous, until in time they present that characteristic uniformity of type to which we have referred above. In the instances I have dealt with in the foregoing, it may indeed be questioned whether the different racial elements brought into contact had merely come into juxta-position or superposition, without blending from the anthropological standpoint; but in other in-stances such fusion seems indisputable. The great races of mankind appear, in fact, to be the product of such fusion (13).

European races, or races of European origin, un-doubtedly offer us the best that the human species has so far produced. Now, among these races the pigmentation of eyes and hair which display—albeit with varying frequency—all gradations from blue to brown and from fair to black, respectively, and even the form of the hair, which varies from absolute straightness to the thickly curled variety, are indisputable evidence of the fusion of diverse racial elements, dating from prehistoric times. The most advanced of the yellow races, the Japanese, are held to be an amalgam of different racial elements, probably some like the Manchu and the South Chinese, and another Malayan or Oceanian, besides the paleoasiatic element contributed by the Ainu. Likewise, among the Malay races the Javanese stand out from the rest by reason both of their recent demographic development and of their distinctive artistic production. And this people is the product of a combination of diverse anthropological elements, among which we must certainly count Malay and Indian. The demographic decadence of many African populations is in sharp contrast with the expansion of the Bantu race, which causes anxiety to the white supremacy in South Africa. And the Bantus are also regarded as a product of crossings between Negroes and Hamites which must have taken place about 2000 years B.C.

An exhaustive study from this standpoint of the several regions of different countries would be of the highest interest. As regards Italy, an inquiry which I carried out regarding the cephalic index of soldiers belonging to the several departments (14), and the results of which have been later confirmed by Boas (15), revealed the fact that the greatest

toes, have no doubt attracted particular attention to themselves owing to their numbers and distinctive appearance, and there may have been a tendency to extend to all half-bloods the unfavorable opinion which they seem to deserve (20). On the other hand, other hybrid races seem to be particularly well favored. This seems to be true of the hybrids of Rehoboth, whom Eugene Fischer studied so carefully before the war. These people, the offspring of Dutch colonials and Hottentots, formed before the war a practically independent republic. Now, while in respect of many characters they seem to be intermediate between the two parent-races, in others, and more especially in stature, frugality, and resistance to fatigue and illness, they are superior to them both (21).

The copious data and evidences published by several authors show similar results for the crosses between Whites and Indians in the United States (22). Crossings between some Oceanian populations and Whites or Chinese show also products superior, from some points of view, to their parents (23). On the other hand, the studies so far made for hybrids resulting from intercourse between Europeans and Malayans do not seem to offer characteristics notably superior or inferior to those of the parent-races (24).

The different results of crossbreeding are confirmed by the study of the population of Brazil, where many races of Iberian, Italian, German, Slav, Syrian, and Japanese origin have mixed and mix, almost unchecked by race prejudice, on the one hand with the Negroes, formerly imported and who have since multiplied to a great extent, and on the other hand with the aborigines. On the whole it cannot be said that the offspring of these crossings are superior to the offspring of the original races. In many cases a contrary impression is given (25). But there is one state, that of Ceará, whose population, resulting from intercourse between Europeans and the natives, is said to be characterized by physical resistance and by psychic qualities of daring, frugality, and tenacity which are not found in the native populations and are not common in the Brazilians of European descent. The half-castes of Ceará are also, according to the evidence of persons well acquainted with the demographic conditions of those populations, extremely prolific, and the multiple births seem to be exceptionally frequent among them (26). This is one of the cases in which we may wonder if we are in the presence of a new and vital race destined to expand on the South American continent (27).

For a new race to gain ground, it must not only

possess the physical and mental qualities which assist it in the struggle for life, or which, at least, enable it to adapt itself to the environment, but it must also have a high birth-rate to assure it the possibility of expanding. Among the other hybrids studied, the half-castes of Rehoboth also are more prolific than either of the two races from which they descend (28). It seems likely that they, too, could have formed the nucleus of a new race had not the World War in the first place, and the contact with civilization afterward, broken down the isolation in which they lived, leading to the dispersion of a great part of the population. Several other crossed races seem also to present a high degree of fertility (29).

On the other hand, the fertility of other mixed or hybrid populations is low, when they are not sterile. Apart from the limited fecundity, to which I have already referred, of mixed marriages in civilized countries (which might be ascribed partly to the fact that in most cases such marriages are between persons of the upper and less prolific classes, and among these they belong to the categories less tied by tradition and less the creatures of instinct, and perhaps also due in part to the less solid nature of the bond), there is a lot of evidence forthcoming on the low fertility of mulattoes (30).

The facts so far adduced indicate that the new races and nations whom we meet in history can only account for a very small portion of the new types produced by racial crossings; they represent the few successful attempts as compared to the vastly greater number which have failed either because the products of the cross were not successful as regards quality, or because they were not sufficiently prolific, or because the hybrids were not adequately subjected to the selective action of the struggle for life, or of sexual competition, or of emigration, which eliminate inferior specimens and dissonant combinations, or else because they went under in the struggle for life.

These conclusions are, moreover, in keeping with those which the long experience of stock and plant breeders suggests. In their case, also, the new breeds obtained are generally the result of crossing, whose progeny, when especially fitted, have been fixed by selection and inbreeding; but only a small number of said crossings have formed the starting-point for a new breed (31). Here again, the offspring is sometimes characterized by inferior resistant powers and poorer quality than their parents; sometimes again, although stronger, they are completely or almost completely sterile, as is the case with the mule; only occasionally, and often only as the result of a long process of selection, a cross is obtained which unites favorable individual characteristics with high reproductive powers (32).

The theory of the evolution of racial stocks which we have set forth in the previous lectures will perhaps enable us to pick up the thread which will guide us between the apparent contradictions of these results. As we have said, the germinal plasm evolves under the more or less slow differentiating action of the environment. And the differentiation can, of course, proceed in diverse directions and with different degrees of intensity. When the crossing brings together germinal plasms which have differentiated in a like or similar direction, it is evident that the effect of this differentiation will not be neutralized in the offspring but will, if anything, be intensified. And this circumstance, sometimes accompanied by want of harmony in the organs and functions of reproduction, frequently causes hybrids to be unprolific or sterile. But it may occur that the differentiation has taken place in the germinal plasm in different directions; and sometimes, in rare cases, in directions which complete each other; and in such cases in the plasm of the crossbreed the differentiations which have taken place in the plasms of the parent-races will be neutralized, conferring on the hybrids, along with other possible characteristics, that plasticity which allows a new race to start on its life-cycle. In such cases the effect of crossbreeding on the races is similar to that periodically obtained by conjugation, which has been rightly described as a "rejuvenation of the plasm." In birth, as well as in development and death, there is therefore a close analogy between what happens for nations and that which takes place in the case of individuals—an analogy which is moreover quite natural, as I pointed out in my first lecture (33).

This helps us to account for the fact that prolific crossbreeds are more frequent in the case of races which are not strikingly differentiated, for in such cases it is not so difficult for specialization to occur in a complementary direction. It would also explain why it frequently happens that new nations arise from the crossing of a superior, civilized, and dominating race with a race still primitive in its mode of life and culture (34). It is legitimate to suppose that what we may call the "intellectual specialization" of the former and the more marked physical activities of the latter, more readily compensate and correct each other, resulting in combinations which are notably fertile in results, not only from the political but also from the demographic standpoint.

Crossbreeding is evidently more likely to occur in immigration countries, not only because the native races often amalgamate with the immigrants but also because the immigrants themselves present, in comparison with the peoples from which they come, a marked heterogeneity.

I have already referred to the purifying and unifying effect of emigration on the peoples who provide emigrants. Their resultant homogeneity contrasts with the heterogeneous character of the emigrants (35). And indeed, it seems only natural that extremes should be very frequent among these latter. As I have said, emigration does not occur casually among the several elements composing a people. The persons who emigrate are those least well suited to the physical and social environment in which they live, not only from the physical but also from the intellectual and moral standpoint. Unbending characters, unwilling to compromise with their conscience in matters of religion or politics; leaders of unsuccessful factions, and the representatives of fallen governments; idealists who have no chance of realizing their great philanthropic schemes in societies living by old crystallized formulas or who cannot there attempt to carry out radical social reforms, provide first-class material for emigration. But emigration also counts in its ranks the poor, the lazy, and the criminal who are expelled or deported, and persons who are morally, if not legally, banned from society. We also find among emigrants eminent men of science, whom the different countries have in all ages striven to secure, side by side with mental deficients seeking the means of livelihood where the struggle for existence is less severe. From the point of view of energy, it is the most enterprising individuals who are most willing to leave their native land; but on the other hand, this spirit of initiative may be driven to an extreme, and give rise to the psychology of the adventurer; so that here again we find among the emigrants desirable and undesirable varieties.

What has just been said from the standpoint of physical, intellectual, and moral qualities also holds good to some extent as regards reproductive capacity. Generally, emigrants are recruited among the members of the most prolific families, both because these feel most severely the pressure of population and also because, at least during its period of maximum expansion, emigration is mainly fed from the lower classes. But on the other hand, it also seems reasonable to admit that members of very small families, and more especially the only sons, emigrate more readily as they are less likely to be detained by those family ties which attach a man to his native land.

It is therefore not surprising that some new nations, more especially the United States, offer, when compared to Europe, a most extensive scale of physical and moral values, which go from the tribes of deficients to the highest expression of intellectual energy. We can recognize among them, on the one hand, descendants of the criminals, the vagabonds, the unemployed, and the beggars deported from England and France; and, on the other, the descendants of the most enterprising and uncompromising families of Ireland, Scotland, England, Germany, and France, for whom the homeland was too narrow, or who could not tolerate limitations placed on their liberty of conscience or the oppression of a foreign ruler or of a hostile party. And we shall also understand how it is that in the impossibility of expecting the race to be purified by the hardships of the struggle for life (the means of which are still too readily attainable), there should be the desire to eliminate by preventive or repressive measures the propagation of the inferior strains.

Immigration countries thus often become the melting-pots of the old races, the anvil on which new races are hammered out. Forged under the hammer of selection they will move up to replace and vivify the races on the downward path of decline.

We can indeed discern various forms in which the revival of a people may take place.

One of the forms is that in which new blood is infused by the introduction of elements belonging to other races. The case is not infrequent, and seems to account for the arrest in the decay of several senescent populations, such as the Esquimaux of Greenland and some of the Maori tribes, and several of the aboriginal tribes or peoples of America (36). This case comes within the category above referred to, with the difference that the revival is frequently not the beginning of a recovery of the vital cycle of such peoples, but only a prolongation of their descending parabola.

More important is the other case of peoples who, more or less suddenly, and without any immediate influence exerted by external races, emerge from the demographic torpor into which they have fallen, and display quite unexpected energy. This is the case of Japan, which, until the middle of the last century, had a stationary population, and since then started a demographic expansion—an expansion, moreover, not limited to the population —of which history affords few examples (37). But other nations also, in different degrees, have offered, or offer, examples of similar phenomena. Such for instance is the case of Italy, Spain, and in general the Latin nations at the time of the organization of national states.

Now, I think that these phenomena of revival can also be explained by crossbreeding. The populations in which these phenomena occur are, generally speaking, those in which different races have lived side by side, sometimes for long periods, whose amalgamation has hitherto been hindered by political barriers, or by psychological resistance, or by legal prohibitions, or by differences of culture or of language. The time comes when these obstacles which kept them apart are eliminated, when they assimilate their respective cultures, intermix on a large scale, and come to form indeed a single nation.

Thus in Japan the revival coincided with the abandonment of the caste system—under which the higher castes boasted a different racial origin and presented also special physical characteristics of their own (38)—and with the adoption of free circulation between the different strata of the population.

This is fundamentally what occurred also in France, Italy, and Spain when they blossomed into new life in the Middle Ages or in the first period of the modern era. The Nordic populations which had invaded the Roman Empire and had settled down as masters in its territory had at first held themselves more or less aloof from the Latin peoples. In a subsequent period, when Latin civilization regained the upper hand and was assimilated by the Germanic elements, the two races gradually amalgamated; and in the course of time a new race was formed which started the evolution of a new nation.

Conditions in Germany have been similar, with the difference that the amalgamation has occurred between the Nordic race and the Slav and Alpine races rather than between Nordic and Latin stocks.

It is obvious that this interpenetration of the juxtaposed or superimposed elements of diverse races cannot take place suddenly or give immediate results. And for this reason the full flowering of the European nations only took place some centuries after the amalgamation of the old with the new racial elements. Similarly, the economic and military progress of Japan made itself most keenly felt only some time after the abolition of the caste system, and seems to be still going forward.

The theory of the fundamentally biological character of these phenomena of revival is favored by the fact that here again it is not generally restricted to the demographic field, but makes itself felt likewise in the other manifestations of life—political, cultural, economic, and military.

We are dealing with a special form of the case, previously considered, when the amalgamation takes place between racial stocks belonging to a nation already unified in language, culture, and sentiment,—racial stocks not recently introduced from abroad, but which, from time immemorial, have been settled in their present locations, without, however, amalgamating completely in the past, either owing to persistent political divisions or to natural geographical isolation or to tenacious regional prejudices.

And here it is proper to consider the present revival taking place in Spain and in Italy—a revival which started before the war but which has been intensified since its close—a revival embracing political, cultural, economic, and military activities. From the demographic standpoint this revival, while inadequate to exclude those nations from the general decline in the birth-rate, at least enables them to retard the process.

We may well ask whether, in the case of Italy at least, this revival is not due to the more thorough amalgamation of the racial stocks of the several regions which has taken place on a large scale only during the last one or two generations, and which is becoming more and more general as a result of closer economic relations, greater facilities for moving about, and better reciprocal knowledge of each other acquired during the war. It was once said by an eminent statesman of the Italian *risorgimento* that now that Italy was made, the next thing to do was to make the Italians. We can give a deeper and wider significance to this remark than the political one given by its author: not only from the point of view of political psychology, but also from the racial standpoint, Italians had to be unified, and that unification, now hastened by the centralizing policy of the government, is beginning to bear its fruits.

If this be the case, then the hope—and more than the hope, the intimate feeling which many have—that the Italian nation is now renewing itself to write new and glorious pages in its history is not without biological foundations.

NOTES

1. For the program of the Italian Committee on Population, see the communication to the Seventeenth Session of the International Institute of Statistics (Cairo, December 29, 1927, to January 5, 1928): "Le Comité Italien pour l'étude des problèmes de la population," in *Bulletin de l'Institut International de Statistique, Le Caire 1928*, pp. 204–6.

2. L. Gumplovicz went so far in his generalizations as to admit that the organized state must necessarily have arisen from the mingling of at least two different hordes, of which one was generally a warrior horde which dominated the other or others. The subsequent unification of the language would lead to a unified culture and at last to the unification of the race. Cf., more especially, *Die sociologische Staatsidee* (Innsbruck: Wagner, 1902), pp. 118–19, and *Der Rassenkampf, Sociologische Untersuchungen*, Zweite Auflage (Innsbruck: Wagner, 1909), especially pp. 181 f., 236 f., 250 f., 354 f., 373 f.

3. See, in this connection, among modern authors, Ralph Linton, in *Publications of the American Sociological Society*, XIX, 74.

There are also authors who attribute the flourishing of a new civilization, consequent on the mingling of two races, solely to the fact that the race having the older culture communicates it to the more biologically vigorous race of conquering barbarians; whereas subsequent crossings between the two would determine the subsequent decline, as the superior race would be impoverished and the hybrids would end by reverting to the older and inferior type. This is the theory dear to the worshipers of the Nordic myth. Such, for instance, would have happened when conquering Nordic races met with the Alpine populations or with the Mediterraneans of Persia, India, Greece, and Italy. Cf., in this connection, more particularly M. Grant, *The Passing of the Great Race* (4th ed.; London: Bell & Sons, 1926), especially pp. 18, 60, 77, 161, 214–16. The theory is fundamentally that of Gobineau, who attributed to repeated crossbreeding also the progressive decline of population. See *Essai sur l'inégalité des races humaines*, "Librarie de Paris," (5th ed.), II, 560–61.

4. Cf. article by G. Elliot Smith, "The Influence of Racial Admixture in Egypt" in *Eugenic Review*, October, 1915.

5. Cf., on this matter, the note on pages 6–7 of my work *I fattori demografici dell'evoluzione delle nazioni* ("Demographic Factors in the Evolution of Nations") (Turin: Bocca, 1911).

6. See Note 20 below.

7. Cf., for certain data on this matter, *Il sesso dal punto di vista*

statistico ("*Sex from the Statistical Point of View*") (Palermo: San-dron, 1908), p. 348.

8. The phenomenon is well known. At the meeting of the International Federation of Eugenic Organizations held in 1928 at Amsterdam Nilsson-Ehle insisted on the need of bearing it in mind in judging the effects of crossbreeding (H. Nilsson-Ehle, *Rassenkreuzung aus allgemein biologischem Gesichtspunkt*, Institut International d'Anthropologie, IIId Session, Amsterdam [Paris: Hourry, 1928], p. 4).

9. The subject is one of the most discussed. The conclusion which a priori seems most plausible is surely the one reached by Davenport and Steggerda in their recent work *Race Crossing in Jamaica* (Carnegie Institution of Washington, 1929) according to which a greater degree of variability in hybrids should be expected only for those characters in which the parent-races differ genetically. This also seems to be confirmed, to some extent, by the results obtained by the two authors, when, in considering 52 characters in which Negroes differ sensibly from pure Whites, it appears that in the case of 29 such characters the variability of the mulattoes exceeds that of both parent-races, in the case of 14 it was intermediate, and for 9 it was inferior to that of either race.

A greater variability of the hybrids is admitted by many authors, based either on theoretical considerations or on observations or on experimental results. For crossbreeding in general, cf., for instance, E. M. East and D. F. Jones, *Inbreeding and Outbreeding* (London: Lippincott, 1919), p. 201, who demonstrate for the *Maize* that in the pure lines obtained by endogamy the variability is less than in the original heterozygotic populations from which the various lines have been deduced (p. 128); W. E. Castle, "Biological and Social Consequences of Race Crossing," *American Journal of Physical Anthropology*, IX, No. 4 (April–June, 1926), 151–53; C. Wissler, "Distribution of Stature in the United States," *Science Monthly*, XVIII, No. 2 (1924), 137–38; L. C. Dunn, "A Biological View of Race Mixture," *Publications of the American Sociological Society*, XIX (1925), 53–55; F. H. Hankins, in the discussion upon the article of Dunn, *ibid.*, p. 58, and in the works *The Racial Basis of Civilisation* (Knopf, 1926) and *An Introduction to the Study of Society* (New York: Macmillan, 1928), p. 126; C. B. Davenport, "Race Crossing in Man," *Institut Int. d'Anthropologie, IIId Session, Amsterdam, September* 20–29, 1927 (Paris: Nourry, 1928), pp. 10–11. More especially as regards crosses between British and the Tahitians of Norfolk Island, studied by H. L. Shapiro, see E. A. Hooton, "Progress in the Study of Race Mixtures with Special Reference to Work Carried on at Harvard University, *"Proceedings of the American Philosophical Society,"* LXV (1926), 319, n. 4; for European and North-American Indian hybrids, see F. Boas, "Anthropologie der nordamerikanischen Indianer, *"Zeitschrift für Ethnologie* (Berlin, 1895) (at p. 383 for the stature and at p. 405 for the width of the face); for Hawaiian-Chinese and Hawaiian-European hybrids see L. C. Dunn, *An Anthropometric Study of Hawaiians of Pure and Mixed Blood* (Cambridge, Massachusetts: Peabody Museum, 1928), pp. 147, 163; for Laplander and Nordic Hybrids, A. Mjoen *Rassenmischung bei Menschen*, Institut Int. d'Anthropologie, IIId Session, Amsterdam, September 20–29, 1927 (Paris: Nourry, 1928), pp. 14–19.

The opposing theory is sustained more especially by M. J. Herskovits, "Variability and Racial Mixture" (*American Naturalist*, LXI [January–February, 1927], 70–76, n. 672; and *The American Negro* [New York: Knopf, 1928]), who contests the greater variability of hybrids on the basis of his own data and those of various other authors. Indeed, in the case of the mixed race of Rehoboth (a cross between Dutch and Hottentots), E. Fischer found a variability in the males higher for 6 characters and lower for 4, and in the females higher for 1 character and lower for 6, than the variability of the same characters in the population of Baden (*Die Rehobother Bastards* [Jena: Fischer, 1913], p. 189). For Sioux Indian and European crossbreeds, Sullivan found that, both for males and females, the variability of 9 out of 21 characters examined was higher, and of 12 lower, than that of the same characters in pure-blood Sioux (L. R. Sullivan, "Anthropometry of the Siouan Tribes," *Anthropological Papers of the American*

POPULATION

Museum of Natural History, XXIII, Part III, 169). Professor Todd has found that, in the case of 100 cadavera of pure Whites and 100 American Negroes, generally of mixed blood, the variability of most of the characters (Herskovits, however, reports data only for sitting height and length of the head) was greater for the latter. W. S. Ossenfort, when examining the skeletons at the Washington University in St. Louis found lower variability among American Negroes (who are mostly mixed) than in Whites. The anthropometric data taken during the last war and elaborated by Davenport and Love give for Negroes (mostly mixed) greater variability as regards stature and weight, but less for chest girth, than in the case of the other nationalities considered who form part of the American population. Finally, Herskovits, for 23 characters, was able to compare the variability of American Negroes (whom he considered largely mixed with Whites and Indians) and that of pure Whites, Negroes, and Indians; and he found that for 10 characters, the variability of the American Negroes was relatively high, for 6 very low, for 7 intermediate. (Cf. *The American Negro*, p. 26.)

Like Fischer and Herskovits, E. Rodenwaldt was led by comparing the variability of the natives of Kisar and that of their European hybrids, both living in the same environment, to conclude that hybrids present no greater degree of variability (*Die Mestizen auf Kisar* [Jena: Fischer, 1928], I, 403–4); but his results, when carefully examined, are more in keeping with an opposite conclusion; I need only state that, of the 48 characters examined, no less than 31 for the males, and 38 for the females, were more variable in hybrids than in Kisarese.

Also as regards researches of Herskovits, we should not overlook the fact that from the data he gives (cf. *The American Negro*, pp. 13–15), we can deduce that the relative variability (calculated on the coefficient of variation) is lower for pure Negroes than for hybrids of various gradations, and this for all the characters for which he furnished the data (width of nostrils, sitting height, thickness of the lips, intensity of the pigmentation), a conclusion confirmed as regards pigmentation by the researches now printed by Miss Irene Barnes ("The Inheritance of Pigmentation in the American Negro," *Human Biology*, September, 1929).

It cannot be disregarded that results as to the comparative variability of the several characters of the parent-races and their hybrids seem to differ from case to case.

It is going too far, in my opinion, to suggest with Herskovits that, in the case of human hybrids, the inheritance of characters cannot be brought within the Mendelian scheme (*The American Negro*, p. 81) (a conclusion also contradicted by the researches of Miss Barnes), although it must certainly be admitted that a multiplicity of factors often renders the inheritance scheme in man more complicated. (See, in this connection, more especially H. E. Ziegler, *Die Vererbungslehre in der Biologie und in der Sociologie* [Jena: Fischer, 1918], p. 134.)

If we do not always find in hybrids that greater variability which might be expected, even with the multiple-factor scheme, this may be due either to the unifying action of severe sexual selection—such as Herskovits has demonstrated in case of American Negroes (*The American Negro*, chap. iv, pp. 51–66), but which it is hard to grant in the case of other hybrid populations (for instance, those of Rehoboth, Kisar, and Jamaica, where probably there is little celibacy)—or to natural selection, which during inter-uterine and extra-uterine growth eliminates extreme variations.

In this connection the remark deserves note that when the half-breeds studied lived in the same environment and under conditions similar to those of the parent-race with which they are compared—as happens in the researches of Rodenwaldt and Davenport—they present a distinctly higher degree of variability to that of the parent-races. The half-breeds of Rehoboth seem, instead, to have lived for many years under particularly hard conditions; and certainly the life of the ancestors of the American Negroes cannot have been a very pleasant one.

It does not seem that we can accept the explanation given by Rodenwaldt according to which all the so-called "pure" races are in reality not only crossed but have already attained the maximum variability of the essential characters of the human species, so that successive crossbreeding between them cannot lead, in the hybrids, to a further increase in variability. This further increase could only occur for those racial characters depending on isolation, as for instance, the color of the skin. As a matter of fact, if this opinion should be well founded, it could only explain why the *range of variation* is not greater among hybrids than among existing races considered pure, but it could not explain why the respective *coefficient of variation* is not higher.

10. Fischer (*op. cit.*, pp. 207–13) found between the various characters of the half-breeds of Rehoboth very low coefficient of correlation, which made him conclude (although he did not possess analogous coefficients for the parent-races) that the character of both parent-races are inherited by hybrids independently the one from the other.

On the other hand, Rodenwaldt, for the half-castes of Kisar, often found high coefficients of correlation between the several characters; and these were sometimes higher (in 5 cases), sometimes equal (in 3 cases), and sometimes lower (in 5 cases) than those found among the natives of Kisar for the same characters (cf. *op. cit.*, pp. 408–12). He admitted that the impression that crossbreeding produces an unusual combination of characters is well founded as far as the less important characters are concerned (*ibid.*, pp. 405–13), but excluded that it could alter the fundamental relations between the more important characters (*ibid.*, p. 413), and reserved any judgment upon the more or less close correlation between the characters of hybrids as compared to those of the purer races, in the absence of sufficient data for the latter (*ibid.*, pp. 413–18).

From Sullivan's data it would appear that the correlation is higher rather than lower among the hybrids as compared to the pure Indians, although, as he himself observed, it is lower in the hybrids for those characters in which the two parent-races differ most (cf. *op. cit.*, pp. 158, 165, 168, 170).

Dunn is quite explicit in his conclusions and affirms that Hawaiian-Chinese and Hawaiian-European half-castes are more variable, principally owing to the formation of new combinations of characters (*An Anthropological Study, etc.*, pp. 163–75).

The results obtained by Davenport and Steggerda are significant: for 9 pairs of characters for which the coefficients of correlation were calculated for Whites, mulattoes and Negroes, the mulatto males showed, in 7 cases the lowest correlations and in 2 the highest, and the females in 5 cases the lowest and in 4 cases intermediate correlations to those between the two pure races (p. 297).

The multiplicity of the combinations of characters of hybrids is admitted by many authors. Cf., for instance, East and Jones (*op. cit.*, pp. 201, 205); Castle (*op. cit.*, p. 151); Hankins (*An Introduction, etc.*, pp. 126, 127). Even Gobineau, so averse to crossbreeding, admitted that it may lead to new characters; and, indeed, in his opinion artistic genius, unknown to the pure races, owed its origin to these combinations (*op. cit.*, I, 218).

I think that in this matter it is especially desirable to distinguish carefully between the combinations to which crossbreeding give rise and those which survive the action of sexual and natural selection. Where such action is severe, it is not surprising that many combinations have been eliminated from the hybrids, especially after a few generations, while in survivors the characters are not less closely correlated than in the pure races.

But it should also be noted that often hybrids are not the product of chance unions among the parent-populations, with whom they are subsequently compared, but of unions between particular homogeneous groups—a circumstance which naturally tends to reduce in the hybrids the variability of the single characters and the multiplicity of the combinations as compared to those of the parent-races considered as a whole.

11. This is the clear impression that I brought back from my visit to Brazil, and from the observation of the Indian half-castes seen in Canada. As far as the racial mixtures in Brazil are concerned, my impression is confirmed by what is stated in the "Eugenical News" by

POPULATION

Dr. Renato Kehl (*Ethnic Elements in the Population of Brazil*, October, 1929). Of the physical, intellectual, and moral disharmonies of hybrids, many writers speak, both old (cf., for instance, Agassiz cited by Davenport and Steggerda, *op. cit.*, p. 469; and Nietzsche cited by Rodenwaldt, *op. cit.*, p. 415) and modern (cf. Fischer, *op. cit.*, pp. 298–99; East and Jones, *op. cit.*, pp. 252–53; Davenport, *The Effects of Race Intermingling*, cited article, pp. 364 ff.; *Race Crossing in Man*, cited article, pp. 12–14; J. A. Mjoen, "Harmonic and Disharmonic Race Crossing," *Eugenics in Race and State* [Baltimore, 1923], pp. 41–61); and *Rassenmischung bei Menschen*, cited article, p. 19; Hooton, *op. cit.*, p. 315; Davenport and Steggerda, *op. cit.*, pp. 470–72).

Nevertheless, other authors contest such impressions and sustain that disharmonies are not more frequent in hybrids, unless by "disharmonies" are meant unusual combinations (for instance, blond hair and dark eyes), which are not, however, the expression of an organic lack of equilibrium and on which natural selection could not act (cf. Castle, *op. cit.*, pp. 150–53; Dunn, "A Biological View, etc.," p. 54; Hankins, *An Introduction to the Study of Society*, p. 125), even if they may offer ground for marriage selection (cf. Rodenwaldt, *op. cit.*, p. 423). As regards disharmonies in the moral sphere, it is known that they are determined or accentuated, at least in many, by the lack of balance between the aspirations of the hybrids to be considered equal to the superior parent-race and the tendency of the latter to keep them apart as inferior beings (cf. Fischer, *op. cit.*, pp. 298–99; Castle, *op. cit.*, p. 154; Hankins, in debate on Dunn's article, "A Biological View of Race Mixture, p. 58, *An Introduction, etc.*, p. 126; D. Simoncelli, *La demografia dei meticci* ("*The Demography of Half-Breeds*") (Sora: Camastro, 1929), pp. 82, 103–4.

We might also inquire whether the disharmonies may be accentuated by the frequent contrast between the intellectual character of the different social classes to which the white fathers and the colored mothers often belong. Similarly, some authors are of the opinion that the nervous instability of hybrids and the prevalence among them of drunkenness, theft, and other social evils may be explained by the low level of their ancestors (cf. Hankins, *An Introduction, etc.*, p. 126; Castle, *op. cit.*, p. 153). To the same circumstances we might attribute the tendency to tuberculosis on which some insist. (Cf. Mjoen and Davenport, at the Congress of Anthropology of Amsterdam, pp. 13–14, 19.)

On the other hand, if we can admit that moral disharmony may be favored in hybrids by the contrast between the various characters of the upper classes to which the white males often belong and the lower ones from which the colored mothers are often taken, it is also reasonable to admit that it may often be due to the even greater contrast between the psychology of the various races, as, for instance, between the ambition, the love of power, and the adventurous spirit of the whites and the idleness, the inconstancy, the lack of self-control and often of adequate intelligence of many colored people. Indeed, bad behavior arising from the conflict of hereditary instincts seems, to Davenport, the worst of the effects of crossbreeding (*Race Crossing in Man*, cited article, p. 14).

Among many impressions, opinions, and interpretations, Davenport and Steggerda have contributed an important observation (although based, as they themselves admit, on a very scanty number of observations). They found that the mulattoes of Jamaica, although on the average superior in intelligence to the Negroes, present a higher percentage of individuals who fail completely in the intelligence tests. The authors attribute this to incapacity on the part of certain individuals to utilize their native endowment (cf. Davenport and Steggerda, *Race Crossing in Jamaica*, pp. 471–72, and the article of the same title published by Davenport in the *Scientific Monthly*, September, 1928, p. 238).

12. Cf. "Les mouvements de population," *Revue d'hygiène*, November, 1927, pp. 806–8.

13. This conclusion of mine has also been reached by adepts of the most various sciences: archaeologists, such as Flinders Petrie (*The Revolutions of Civilisation* [3d ed.; London: Harper, 1922], pp. 114–

17, 122); historians, such as Myres, "The Cause of the Rise and Fall in the Populations of the Ancient World," *Eugenics Review*, April, 1915, p. 28); sociologists, such as Hankins (discussion upon Dunn's article, "A Biological View of Race Mixture," p. 58, and *An Introduction, etc., op. cit.*, p. 126); geneticists, such as East and Jones (*op. cit.*, p. 256).

14. Cf. "Variabilità e mutabilità, contributo allo studio delle distribuzioni e delle relazioni statistiche ("Variability and Mutability, Contribution to the Study of Statistical Distributions and Relations"), *Studi economico-giuridici della R. Università di Cagliari* [Bologna: Cuppini, 1912], p. 31).

15. Cf. Franz Boas and Helene M. Boas, "The Head Forms of the Italians as Influenced by Heredity and Environment," *American Anthropologist*, Vol. XV, No. 2 (April–June, 1913).

16. At the Institute of Statistics of the Royal University of Rome I have started a systematic inquiry into the distribution of famous Italians classified according to epoch and birthplace. The results arrived at up to the present seem to confirm the current impression above referred to.

17. I refer to the popular Venetian proverb:

> "Venetians great lords
> Paduans great doctors
> Vicentini cat-eaters
> Veronesi all crazy, etc."

Cf. G. Pasqualigo, *Raccolia di proverbi veneti* 3d ed.; (Treviso: Zoppelli, 1882), pp. 255–57.

18. Gubbio and Matelica are particularly quoted in this connection.

19. The diverse results of human crossbreeding depending on the parent-races, and the difficulty of generalizations regarding the characters of their products, are particularly recognized by Davenport (*Race Crossing in Man*, cited article, pages 13–14; Dunn, "A Biological View of Race Mixture, p. 55) and Gates ("A Pedigree Study of American Crosses in Canada," *Journal of the Anthropological Institute*, July–December, 1928, p. 529).

20. For a long time it was usual to state that mulattoes were inferior to both parent-races (cf. Davenport and Steggerda, *op. cit.*, p. 469; Fischer, *op. cit.*, pp. 177–78; E. Dodge, "The Mulatto Problem," *Journal of Heredity*, Vol. XVI, No. 8, p. 283; Castle, *op. cit.*, p. 147). In this sense also Schlaginhaufen, "Bastardierung und Qualitätsänderung," *Natur und Mensch*, September, 1920, p. 36—an opinion which at times was extended to all human hybrids. Some authors think that a distinct difference can be described between Negro-English crossbreeds (for instance, those found in Jamaica) and Negro-Spanish or Negro-Portuguese, so frequent in the islands of Cuba, Haiti, and Porto Rico; the former, they say, have less vitality and fertility, while the latter are strong and fertile (cf. E. Fischer, *op. cit.*, p. 178).

An objective criticism of the facts and recent systematic investigations have shown such statements to be exaggerations. It cannot be denied that mulattoes are generally intermediate between the Whites and Negroes, consequently superior on the whole to the latter and inferior as regards most of the characters in which the Whites are superior; superior to the former and inferior to the latter in those few characters in which Negroes excel. Cf., in particular, the researches of Ferguson and Peterson referred to by Kimball Young (*Publications of the American Sociological Society*, XIX, 78) and by Herskovits ("On the Relation between Negro-White Mixture and Standing in Intelligence Tests," *Pedagogical Seminary*, March, 1926, p. 32) and those made by Herskovits himself (*ibid.*, pp. 40–41); but, above all, those of Davenport and Steggerda, (*op. cit.*, p. 477). It should be noted that this seems to be more especially true for the half-castes of Jamaica to whom the observations of Davenport and Steggerda refer.

The individual successes and the social duties discharged by mulattoes as compared to Whites and Negroes confirm this conclusion. Cf. for instance, Reuter, *The Hybrid as a Sociological Type,"* *Publications of the American Sociological Society*, XIX, 67; Simoncelli, *op. cit.*, p. 25; Castle, *op. cit.*, p. 155.

The ostracism to which mulattoes are subjected in some coun-

POPULATION

tries, sometimes by both parent-races, and almost everywhere by the white race, can, on the other hand, account for some of their defects from the social standpoint. (Cf. in this respect, A. Torres cited by Kehl in *Eugenical News*, October, 1929, p. 149; Simoncelli, *op. cit.*, pp. 25–82; Hankins, *An Introduction*, etc., p. 126; Castle, *op. cit.*, p. 156; Dodge, *op. cit.*, p. 283). At the same time, the individual characters of the parents, which may not correspond to those of the population as a whole, must at times be taken into consideration in a comparative estimate of the characters of hybrids. (Cf. Hankins, *An Introduction*, etc., p. 126; Linton, *op. cit.*, pp. 66–67; Dodge, *op. cit.*, p. 283).

But when all this is admitted, we cannot disregard the fact that, notwithstanding isolated assertions due probably to injustifiable generalizations (for instance, East and Jones, speaking of the extraordinary physical vigor shown by mulattoes [*op. cit.*, p. 252]), no trace has been found in mulattoes of heterosis, i.e., of those manifestations of greater strength, precocity, or vital resistance which characterize many hybrids in the animal and vegetable kingdoms, and also, as we shall see, certain human hybrids (cf. Davenport and Steggerda, *op. cit.*, p. 447), except perhaps for a certain precocity in the intellectual development of children, which, however, does not generally last beyond adolescence (cf. Davenport and Steggerda, *op. cit.*, p. 472; Simoncelli, *op. cit.*, p. 81).

The fact that the crossing of Whites and Negroes produces types more closely resembling the latter than the former in almost all characters (cf. Davenport and Steggerda, *op. cit.*, pp. 460–62) can be explained—rather than by a tendency to revert to the inferior races, which some authors admit (cf. particularly Grant, *op. cit.*, pp. 18, 77) —by the prevalence of Negro characters due to the greater proportion of Negro blood since crossing is more frequent between mulattoes and Negroes than between mulattoes and Whites (see Davenport and Steggerda, *op. cit.*, pp. 462–63); but on the other hand, it is significant that, while mulattoes present a higher percentage than Negroes of individuals who are unsuccessful at the intelligence tests, they do not present an equal or higher frequency than do the Whites of particularly gifted individuals (cf. the data and diagrams given in the work of Davenport and Steggerda). So that we are forced to the conclusion that the crossbreeding of Whites and Negroes gives unfavorable results. Unfavorable and indeed inferior to both parent-races are, according to Mjoen, the results of crossbreeding between Norwegians and Eskimoes (cf. in particular the cited works, "Harmonic and Disharmonic Race Crossings" in *Eugenics in Race and State;* and *Rassenmischung bei Menschen*), who also seem to present a particular predisposition to tuberculosis (data to this effect were communicated also at the last meeting [September, 1929] of the International Federation of Eugenic Organizations; cf. *Eugenical News,* November, 1929, p. 159). Likewise inferior, according to Davenport, are the products of crossbreeding represented by the Eurasians of India (*Race Crossing in Man*, cited article, p. 13) and perhaps also the first generation of European and Australian hybrids ("Notes in Physical Anthropology of Australian Aborigines and Black-White Hybrids," *American Journal of Physical Anthropology*, January–March, 1925, p. 83).

21. Cf. Fischer, *op. cit.*, pp. 134, 176, 177.

22. Cf. F. Boas, "Anthropologie der nordamerikanischen Indianer," p. 353; L. R. Sullivan, "Anthropometry of the Siouan Tribes," p. 171. Reference to phenomena of heterosis in hybrids of French Canadians and American Indians, can be found in Davenport, *Race Crossing in Man*, cited article, p. 13, and Castle, *op. cit.*, p. 155. A very favorable opinion is also given by R. R. Gates on the hybrids of the Whites (of French and British origin) and Indians (Cree and Ojibway) examined by him in northern Ontario (Canada): "A Pedigree Study of Amerindian Crosses, etc.," pp. 529–30. Very important are the data given in the chapter "Fecundity and Vitality" in the volume *Indian Population in the United States and Alaska, 1910* (Washington: Bureau of the Census, 1915). From these it appears that couples of pure Indian blood present a lower percentage of surviving children than do couples in which one or both of the spouses are of mixed

blood. The doubt remains, however, that the difference may be due to diversity of environment (cf. pp. 158–59).

23. European and Tahitian hybrids of Norfolk Island studied by Shapiro, while they do not reveal any physical inferiority, are superior to the parent-races for stature and cephalic diameter (cf. Hooton, *op. cit.*, p. 319). Hawaiian-European and Hawaiian-Chinese hybrids, while they do not reveal pronounced heterosis in their physical measurements, are certainly not inferior. Indeed, according to more than one observer, Hawaiian-Chinese hybrids represent an advance over the types of the parents (Dunn, "A Biological View of Race Mixture," p. 54, and *An Anthropometric Study, etc.*, pp. 147–48). Also, the first generation of white and Hawaiian hybrids showed undoubted superiority in weight and probable superiority in stature (Dunn, *An Anthropometric Study, etc.*, p. 153). R. Goldschmidt has made a brief report on the hybrids of the Bonin Islands, arising from unions first of Polynesian and then of Japanese women with English, American, Negro, and mulatto men ("Die Nachkommen der alten Siedler auf den Bonin Inseln," *Die Naturwissenschaften*, 15 Jahrg., Heft 21). The hybrids give a very good impression both from the point of view of physique and customs.

As regards death-rate, complete life-tables for Whites, Hawaiians, and their half-breeds have been published (cf. H. W. Kung, "Life Tables for Various Groups in Hawaii," *American Journal of Hygiene*) which show that the death-rate for half-breeds is intermediate between that of both parent-races but nearer to the much lower death-rate of the Whites during the growing period and in adult age, and nearer to that of the Hawaiians in old age (cf., in particular, p. 105). The article does not give facts from which to determine whether, as is probable, and to what extent, the differences can be attributed to social factors. Lastly, as regards fertility, Pitt Rivers refers that the Maoris often assert that their women are more fertile when mated to Europeans than to their own stock (cf. *The Clash of Culture and the Contact of Races* [London: Routledge, 1927], p. 223).

As regards resistance to tuberculosis (to which mulattoes are, as we have seen, said to be more susceptible than Negroes), the half-castes of Polynesians and Europeans are less so than the natives, according to Bordier; and quatroons are still more resistant (cf. G. Sanarelli, *Tubercolosi ed evoluzione sociale* ("*Tuberculosis and Social Evolution*") [Milan: Treves, 1913], p. 130).

24. The Kisar half-castes from Whites and Malayans, accurately studied by Rodenwaldt, do not show, according to that author, traces of heterosis, but rather organic impoverishment (cf. *op. cit.*, pp. 127, 140, 148, 158, 164, 189, 420).

It is curious that so little information exists about the hybrids of Europeans and Asiatics. During the discussion which followed the papers of Nilsson-Ehle, Davenport, and Mjoen at the International Congress of Anthropology at Amsterdam (1927), Peake asserted that he had met some fine specimens of hybrids of Europeans and Asiatic parentage but that, of all those he had come across, he knew no more admirable groups than the people of Dutch and Singhalese extraction, known in Ceylon as "Dutch Burgers" (cf. vol. cit. at p. 21). It may be well to remember here that Gobineau considered the Malayan race (or, as he said, the Malayan variety) the result of a cross between the yellow and black races, and admitted that it was superior in intelligence to both parent-races (*op. cit.*, p. 218). Upon the accuracy of this assertion, both as regards the origin of the Malayan race and its intellectual superiority as compared to the yellow race, some more than justifiable doubts may be expressed, but the passage is in any case interesting, as it shows that even such a radical opponent of crossbreeding as Gobineau admits that in some cases it gives rise to results superior to the parent-races.

25. This impression of mine agrees with that of Dr. R. Kehl lately expressed in *Eugenical News*, October, 1929.

26. Dr. de Bulhoes Carvalho, General Director of Statistics in Brazil, confirms this information in his letter to me, dated May 4, 1928: "La fecondité des habitants de Ceará est un fait courant dans cette région source d'une émigration assez nombreuse à laquelle est dû le peuplement du territoire de l'Acre et de quelques autres régions

de la vallée de l'Amazone. Il est à regretter que la statistique ne puisse exercer dans les conditions actuelles, un contrôle effectif sur les naissances de Cearà pour en dresser des relevés complets qui mettraient, à mon avis, en évidence la fréquence des accouchments multiples sur lesquels, plus d'une fois, a été appelée mon attention, par les agents censitaires, à l'occasion du recensement de 1920." The *Annuario Estadistico do Cearà for 1924* (Fortaleza, 1928) enables us, anyhow, to see, even though it be only approximately, the high fecundity of this people. In 1924, 63,765 infants were baptized (p. 70), which, compared to the population in 1920, given as 1,319, 228 inhabitants, would correspond to a birth-rate of over 48 °/oo. Between 1920 and 1924 the population probably increased: Dr. de Bulhoes, in one of his handwritten communications, placed it in 1923 at 1,421,514 inhabitants, for which the 63,765 baptized would represent a birthrate of 45 °/oo. But, on the other hand, it is known that some of the children die before christening, so that we may conclude that the birth-rate of the state of Cearà exceeds 45 °/oo.

27. As has been noted in connection with mulattoes, so in the case of hybrids generally, their qualities depend directly on the characters of the individuals of both races which cross—characters which, in their turn, depend on the average or typical characters of the race and on the deviations which the individuals considered present in respect to such type or average. It is thus evident that the fact that polygamy prevails among the conquering Mohammedans, especially among the chiefs, generally possessing superior physical and intellectual gifts, was not without influence on the characters of the descendants born of the native women received into the harem. It also explains why the mixture between natives and the immigrants of a given race may give different results in the first and in the last periods of immigration, as very often the emigrants from a nation are the result of a selection of a different and sometimes an opposite kind in the first period and in successive ones. The physical, mental, and moral characteristics of the Portuguese who conquered Brazil and the East Indies were certainly very different from those of the present

emigrants of the same nation. Rightly Reuter, Linton, and Young, in judging the comparative value of hybrids and their progenitors in the mixtures of races in North America, are trying to ascertain the importance of the selection which may have taken place at the various epochs in the case of the white fathers on the one hand and the Negro or Indian mothers on the other (cf. the cited articles of these authors in the *Publications of the American Sociological Society*, XIX, 64–66, 73–74, 78).

It is also very likely that in the crossbreeds of pure races, as happens with many crosses in plants and animals, reciprocal crosses may produce different results; and, from this point of view, the well-known fact, to which Reuter rightly calls attention (cited article, p. 64) may assume importance, i.e., that most human crosses occur between males of a superior race—if not intrinsically, at least politically and socially—and females of an inferior race and are generally the result of illegitimate unions. As far as I know, the problem of reciprocal crosses between human races has not yet been studied.

The different results of crossbreeding undoubtedly depend, and in essential ways, on the more or less hostile, or per contra favorable social environment in which the hybrids are brought up and develop. The best proof of this is that the results obtained from crossing the same races differ profoundly, depending on whether the hybrids are brought up by a race which despises them or by one which holds them in consideration. (See in this respect, above all, Linton, cited article, p. 74; Simoncelli, *op. cit.*, pp. 25, 65, 87, 89–91, 103–4; Castle, *op. cit.*, p. 147).

And lastly, we must note that in speaking of the good or bad results of crossbreeding it is always necessary to refer to a determined environment. Authors, even among those least favorable to crossbreeding between Whites and Negroes, recognize, nevertheless, that the mulattoes are more resistent to certain diseases and to tropical climates than the Whites (cf. East and Jones, *op. cit.*, p. 254; Simoncelli, *op. cit.*, pp. 26, 44, 83, 110; Davenport, *Scientific Monthly*, September, 1928, p. 238) and that, in comparison with Negroes, they are intellectually superior. This combination of characters may be considered as insufficient to compensate the many superiorities of the Whites in the temperate and cold climates, but it may bestow a decisive advantage over the Whites in tropical climates. Crosses between Whites and Negroes may therefore be considered disadvantageous in the United States of America and yet on the contrary be advantageous in the basin of the Amazon and in equatorial Africa. On the advantages of crossbreeding for populating colonies, see, in particular, Simoncelli (*op. cit.*), who devotes two chapters to the question of half-castes in the colonies in relation to colonization.

28. The average number of children ascertained by Fischer for the half-castes of Rehoboth was 7.7 per marriage. In marriages between the Cape Dutch, the average is said to have been 6.3 (or something more, as those who died before baptism were not taken into account). Among the Hottentots the average is approximately 6 (cf. Fischer, *op. cit.*, pp. 125–27). For other evidence of the high degree of fertility of the crosses between Hottentot women and white or Negro men, see Simoncelli, *op. cit.*, p. 7, and Fischer, *op. cit.*, p. 127.

29. In the half-castes of Kisar, Rodenwaldt found an average of 7.3 children per marriage in the marriages of the last two generations (*op. cit.*, p. 304). Simoncelli reports from various authors as an example of half-caste populations of high fecundity, the results of unions between Whites and Indians and between Indians and Negroes in South America (*op. cit.*, pp. 7, 12), between Polynesians and British in the Pitcairn Islands (*ibid.*, pp. 14–15), and between Malayans and Europeans at Java (p. 14). Other proofs, such as the prevalence of half-castes over pure-blooded individuals in certain populations (for instance, in the Philippines, in the Antilles, and in Guiana), also recorded by Simoncelli (*op. cit.*, p. 12), are not, however, free from objections, as the number of half-castes may increase solely owing to the increasing number of mixed unions. Hankins (*An Introduction, etc.*, p. 126) and Linton (*op. cit.*, p. 73) admit that, in general, human hybrids are as fertile as, and even more so than, the pure races, without, however, stating to what data or to what races they refer. Such gen-

eral statements may, however, fall into error, as we shall see below. Special importance attaches to the data for marriages of pure-blooded Indians and for mixed marriages or marriages of hybrids, contained in the cited volume *Indian Population in the United States and Alaska*, which clearly show a higher percentage of sterility and a lower fecundity in the case of pure-blooded Indians (cf. pp. 157–58). Among hybrid population of high fecundity the fertility of the various cross-breeds may differ according to the races. Hembron, for instance, cited by Simoncelli (*op. cit.*, p. 7), found the fecundity of Indian females of South America with Whites and with Negroes higher than with Indians; but with Whites it was much higher than with Negroes. On the contrary, in the United States and Alaska neither the marriages of the Indians with Negroes nor those between half-castes when at least one of the spouses has Negro blood are more sterile or less productive than the marriages between Whites and Indians or between hybrids of Whites and Indians (cf. *ibid.*, pp. 157–58).

30. Cf., on this point, the various authors cited by Simoncelli, *op. cit.*, pp. 9–11, and by Davenport, *Heredity of Skin Color in Negro-White Crosses* (Washington: Carnegie Institution, 1913), p. 46. It is true that Davenport contests the basis of such assertions by noting that the marriages between mulattoes studied by him (21) had an average of 4.4 children, equal to that for all the marriages considered. But it should be noted in the first place that 4.4 is not a high average and, in the second place, that in all or almost all of the marriages considered by him either both spouses were colored (hybrids of Whites and Negroes) or one colored and the other White or Negro; so that if 4.4 be considered a low average, the only conclusion that can be drawn is that the fertility of the unions of crosses of Whites and Negroes among themselves or with each parent-race is not high. This conclusion seems to be confirmed by the examination of the nuptial fecundity of the Negro populations of the various states of the "registration area," which I had the opportunity of calculating for a work now on hand. The ratio of legitimate births to the married women between fifteen and fifty years of age is for the Negroes in all the states

lower than that of the white population, which is anything but high. Still more considerable is the difference, according to Tait's index, which is a more accurate index of nuptial fecundity than the foregoing ratio, for it takes into consideration the average age of the married women, which for the Negroes is always lower than for Whites. The data are based upon the legitimate births in the two years 1919–20 and upon the married women considered in the census of 1920. In order to give an idea of the nuptial fecundity of Negroes, I give below the contemporary data (1920 or 1921) for some other countries.

STATE	LEGITIMATE BIRTHS PER 1,000 MARRIED WOMEN FROM 15 TO 50 YEARS			TAIT'S INDEX		
	White	Negro	Yellow	White	Negro	Yellow
California.............	92	79	....	0.66	0.49	
Connecticut...........	155	130	....	1.01	0.78	
Indiana...............	126	82	....	0.80	0.48	
Kansas...............	132	88	....	0.83	0.54	
Kentucky.............	161	91	....	0.96	0.54	
Maryland.............	146	132	....	0.92	0.78	
Massachusetts.........	154	134	....	1.03	0.83	
Michigan.............	144	80	....	0.90	0.43	
New York............	136	103	....	0.89	0.60	
North Carolina........	201	179	....	1.18	1.00	
Ohio.................	122	90	....	0.77	0.51	
Pennsylvania..........	156	97	....	0.99	0.56	
South Carolina........	181	153	....	1.05	0.84	
Virginia..............	174	162	....	1.06	0.95	
Canada...............	130	....	....	0.84		
Chili.................	230	....	....	1.39		
Japan (1925)..........	....	....	199	....	....	1.20
Australia.............	171	....	....	1.14		
South African Union....	191	....	....	1.28		
Ireland (1911).........	251	....	....	1.82		
England..............	149	....	....	1.08		
France...............	137	....	....	0.95		
Austria...............	150	....	....	1.13		
Italy.................	220	....	....	1.48		
Greece...............	161	....	....	1.09		
Norway..............	207	....	....	1.43		
Russia (1897)..........	298	....	....	1.74		

The comparison between these data shows how low is the nuptial fecundity of the Negroes. When we remember that most American Negroes are really of mixed blood (only 22 per cent are pure-blooded, according to the researches of Herskovits, *The American Negro*, p. 9), we may conclude that there is some truth in the impressions of those who declare that the unions of Negroes with Whites are not very fertile.

The crosses between Negroes and Whites do not seem to be the only ones showing low fertility. The same is true, according to T. Guevana, of the marriages between Spaniards and Araucanes (Indians of Chile). From the data of this author reported by Simoncelli (*op. cit.*, pp. 75–76) it appears that 58 marriages between Araucanes and Spaniards gave on the average 2.2 children, and the percentage of childless marriages was almost 40 per cent; whereas 246 American families presented an average of 2.8 children, with no percentage of childless marriages. The difference, as regards childlessness, is so striking and in such sharp contrast with the evidence given by other authors of the high fertility of unions between Europeans and other Indian populations that, before accepting it, it would be well to examine whether the data for the two categories of marriages are really comparable. It should be noted that, if the childless marriages are eliminated, the average number of children would be higher for the mixed marriages (3.6 against 2.8).

31. The conclusion come to by geneticists with the help of the Mendelian theory from series of well-organized experiments have confirmed in detail and explained, at least to some extent, the observations of breeders. To purify in segregation, with the help of endogamy and selection, the lines obtained from crossings in order to cross again the pure lines so obtained and then start the cycle over again, seems by common consent the best way to obtain new forms and improve existing ones. (Cf. Babcock and Clausen (*Genetics in Relation to Agriculture* [New York: McGraw Hill, 1927],pp. 597, 601; East and Jones, *op. cit.*, pp. 202, 212. Eminent archaeologists and historians express the same opinion as regards human races. Cf. Flinders Petrie, *op. cit.*, p. 131; J. L Meyers, *op. cit.*, p. 28.) Some think we should seek here for the origin of domestic animals and cultivated plants, both of which should be considered as hybrids of different forms or species which

have undergone a process of selection (cf., in particular, East and Jones, *op. cit.*, p. 210).

The observation of the reproductive processes met with in nature, particularly in plants, shows, moreover, that these things behave as though nature tried to assure, at least from time to time, the possibility of crossbreeding, and this would be the reason for the prevalence of sexual reproduction. (Cf. also on this point, East and Jones, *op. cit.*, pp. 31–35, 98, 114, 195, 201, 209). Indeed, some authors, certainly exaggerating (as it is not possible to deny the importance of mutations), admit that in nature new forms always arise from crossbreeding, some being eliminated by selection while others survive, forming the species (J. P. Lotsy, *Evolution by Means of Hybridization* [The Hague: Nijoff, 1916]).

It is hardly necessary to note the support that all these facts and proofs give to our cyclic theory of the evolution of populations. For that theory leads close observers to the conclusion that matters proceed with the human species as they do in nature, in the domestication and in the scientific rearing of plants and animals. Apart from the appearance of mutations, not only the dominating races of mankind, as we have seen above, but all races, derive their origin from crossbreeding. The group feeling determined by physical, or social, or cultural, or administrative factors (race, cast, city, state, etc.) and the hostility of neighboring groups, acts as an isolating factor, and in isolation the complete fusion of races which have been thus mingled gradually takes place. In this consists the biological function of the group feeling. When isolation continues for a long time, decadence sets in, the only remedy for which would be the fusion of new blood brought about by the invasion of new races from which, under the same or some other name, a new ethnic unity would arise, starting a new cycle. All the human races, as is often asserted today, would, therefore, be crossed in the sense that all have arisen from recent or remote crossings. In this sense there would be no originally pure races, but only purified races, which, however, cannot continue indefinitely, as, after reaching a certain degree of homogeneity, they would end by decaying if they were not renewed by new crossbreeding. Thus the cyclic process of evolution which occurs in the human races, if at first it may seem a wasteful system, inasmuch as it implies periodical recovery and dispersion of energy, really, under the biological laws governing organic life, corresponds to the ideal system suggested by the most modern results of genetics.

32. It is possible that the divergent results may depend on the greater or lower genetic diversity of the parents. When these are very similar, the effect of the crossing cannot be noted; but the favorable results are evident and accentuate themselves as the difference increases, until they attain the optimum above which effects cease to be favorable and become unfavorable. There is a limit beyond which reproduction, and then union, becomes impossible. East and Jones distinguish various stages in plants, among which there are, naturally, gradations: (1) the parents are so alike that no appreciable effect can be noted from crossing; (2) the hybrids are equally, if not more, fertile and vigorous than both the parent races; (3) the hybrids are equally or more vigorous than the parents, but less fertile or even sterile, except at times with one or other of the parent races; (4) the hybrids are weaker than the parent-races and incapable of reproduction; (5) the crossing gives rise to a product, but it is incapable of development; (6) the parents are so different that crossing is impossible. The same stages occur with animals, with the difference that categories (4) and (5) happen very rarely, as in animals, when offspring are obtained, they are usually just as vigorous or more so than the parents (*op. cit.*, pp. 162–63, 191–94). Both for animals and plants, according to East and Jones, the optimum is therefore attained, first as regards fertility and afterward as regards bodily development—a wise provision to prevent crossing from being a source of deterioration to the species.

The observations above reported, relating to human races, do not however reveal very clearly this order of precedence. The classification given by East and Jones should be considered solely as an outline, for it is certain that the reality is much more complex. It is also certain that the possibility of hybridization between two forms is not always a sure sign of their relationship (cf. E. B. Babcock and R. E. Clausen, *op. cit.*, chap. xxvii, "Interspecific Hybridization," pp. 304 ff.), even if it may be considered as such for practical purposes. (Cf. R. Goldschmidt, *Einführung in den Vererbungswissenschaft* [Berlin: Springer, 1928], pp. 384–85.)

33. Another explanation might be given of the rejuvenation of nations, consequent on racial crossing, and their subsequent evolution, i.e., the same explanation advanced by those geneticists most faithful to the Mendelian theory to explain, on the one hand, the heterosis of hybrids and, on the other, the decadence which occurs, both in size and vitality as well as in fertility of the lines progressively purified by endogamy. Endogamy, by progressively increasing the percentage of the homozigotic individuals, reveals lethal factors, or at least factors unfavorable to individual development and to reproduction, which, as they are recessive, were originally latent in each of the isolated strains. The influence of endogamy—more or less unfavorable according to the quantity and quality of the latent factors originally present in the isolated strain—exhausts itself in the course of the generations required to obtain a complete homozigotic population, some ten generations in the extreme case of endogamy presented by self-fertilization. Vice versa, in hybrids of the first generation, heterozigotic in all their characters, the action of lethal or unfavorable factors present in a race, in so far as they are recessive and do not find corresponding factors in the other race, would remain disguised by the dominating factors present in the latter, but this advantage would be attenuated in the second generation in a degree corresponding to the reduction of the percentage of heterozigotic individuals, and the attenuation, according to these authors, would be progressively accentuated in successive generations (cf. East and Jones, *op. cit.*, pp. 80–210, Babcock and Clausen, *op. cit.*, pp. 215–18, 398–400, 406–16, 575–84, 591–95; R. Goldschmidt, *Einführung, etc.*, pp. 349–59).

In substance this is the theory followed by Davenport to explain the cycles of development of the populations of ancient Egypt and of ancient Greece and Rome described by Flinders Petrie (cf. C. H.

Davenport, *The Effects of Race Intermingling*, cited article [1917], pp. 367–68, who, however, attributes to Flinders Petrie much more than he said or at least than he says in the third edition [1922] of his work).

Even in its application to scientific experiments on hybrids this explanation is not exempt from objections. Indeed, if the recessive quality of the lethal or unfavorable factors can explain the heterosis of hybrids of the first generation as compared to numbers of the parent-races, and the decline of heterosis from the first to the second generation, it cannot, however, explain (at least in the form in which the explanation is given) the further and progressive reduction of heterosis which occurs in the subsequent generations, which should, on the contrary, remain stationary. (The contrary assertion of East and Jones, *op. cit.*, p. 177, is probably based on a material error of calculation.)

Moreover, when transferred to the field of nations, the explanation encounters other obstacles which are not easily overcome.

a) It does not explain the divergent, indeed opposite, results, arising from crossings between the various human races. Why should the hybrids of Norwegians and Eskimoes be inferior, while those of Europeans and Indians are superior, to both parent-races? Why should crossings of Europeans with Australians and with Negroes give unfavorable results while those of Europeans with Hottentots and Hawaiians are favorable? Neither the more or less close relationship of the parent-races nor the more or less marked diversity of single characters—a necessary condition, some say, for the manifestation of heterosis—can explain it.

b) It is absolutely inadmissible to compare populations of millions, such as those of ancient Egypt, Greece, and Rome, and still more so of modern states, with a pure line bred under endogamous conditions.

c) The decline in vigor of the nations, which seems to follow the determination of their anthropological homogeneity, does not cease after a certain number of generations, but on the contrary seems to be accentuated, rendering their equilibrium even more unstable.

POPULATION

34. This, according to Gumplovicz, is the origin of the state. Cf. note 2 of this lecture.

35. Cf., in this connection, our lectures upon "Population Policies" held at the Rome University (Faculty of Political Sciences, 1927–28) (*Population Policies* [Rome: Castellani], chap. xiii), which deal with "Crossings and the Formation of New Races" and contain, in summary, the ideas set forth in this lecture.

36. Cf. for the Eskimoes, G. Carega, "Alcuni dati demografici sugli Esquimesi" ("Some Demographic Data on Eskimoes"), *Metron*, Vol. VII, No. 3 [1928]), for the Maoris, G. H. Lane-Fox Pitt-Rivers, *The Clash of Culture and the Contact of Races*, pp. 75–76, 271–72, Appendix I, pp. 279–82), who extends his conclusions to all the populations of the Polynesian and the Malayan archipelagoes (cf. p. 271), and for the Indians of the United States of America and Alaska the cited volume, *Indian Population, etc. A Study on the Aborigines of Central and South America* (*Studio sugli aborigeni dell'America Centrale e Meridionale*) by Corrado Leopardi, of the Institute of Statistics of the Rome University, comes to the conclusion that these races also tend to disappear, making room for a half-breed race. It is the development of this latter which gives the impression of an increase of the native population. (In the same connection, cf. F. Savorgnan, "Intorno al problema dell'estinzione dei popoli selvaggi ["The Problems of the Extinction of Savage Peoples"] *Rivista di antropologia*, XXVIII [1928–29], p. 7.)

37. The article by J. E. Orchard, "The Pressure of Population in Japan," in *Geographical Review*, July, 1928, contains, besides many interesting particulars, a graph showing the movement of population in Japan from 1720 to our day.

38. The first travelers who reached Japan described as frequent in the upper classes a dolichocephalic type with Semitic features of whom there are today just a very few examples. Cf. "Il diverso accrescimento delle classi sociali e la concentrazione della ricchezza" ("The Different Growth of the Social Classes and the Concentration of Wealth"), *Giornale degli economisti*, January, 1909, p. 65.

POPULATION AND THE FOOD SUPPLY

By SHIROSHI NASU

I. THE STANDARD OF LIVING AND THE POPULATION PROBLEM

I

The standard of living is the pivot on which the population problem rotates. What is called "overpopulation" or "underpopulation" is quite meaningless without reference to the standard of living, because the capacity of a certain society to support a certain number of people is entirely dependent upon the standard of living which its members maintain. Where there is suffering from overpopulation, more people might be sustained only if they were willing to lower their standard of living.

Where then does overpopulation exist? In my opinion it exists whenever there are more people than can be supported by a given society without lowering the average standard of living of the masses. This so-called "superfluous population" or overpopulation may manifest itself in the form of an increase of unemployment, in the lowering of the purchasing power of wages, or in the excessive subdivision of farm lands into ever smaller and smaller allotments. Sometimes people will endeavor to maintain their present standard of living even though they are not receiving sufficient income to enable them to do so. In such cases their fortunes are naturally depleted. The same may happen with national income. A nation may continue or sometimes may even raise its standard of living by consuming the capital which should properly be used for productive purposes. But such a state of affairs cannot continue forever. It will eventually result in reduced production and lessened income, with an inevitable decline in the standard of living.

II

The foregoing argument will be quite clear if we take the simple case of a group of people who are engaged in a single industry. On the other hand if we take the case of several groups engaged in different occupations, as, for example, agriculture and industry, the solution is not so simple. The standard of living in one group may be going up while that in another may be going down; and in this case it will not be so easy to judge whether there is or is not overpopulation in the whole society including both groups. The question arises whether it is proper to look upon the average standard of living of these different groups of people as the test of overpopulation. This question I would answer in the affirmative.

This will be explained in the following manner.

We may see the lowering of the standard of living in a certain section of society, which suggests the existence of overpopulation in that section, while the general average of the standard of living of that society as a whole may be going up. In such a society the particular class or profession which has been overcrowded will gradually lose some of its members, and thus by decreasing the number of participants in a certain business or profession the standard of living of the group will be raised again without impairing too seriously the well-being of people belonging to other groups. Therefore, I believe that even when thinking of the whole society consisting of different classes of people, we may safely take the general average of the standard of living, excluding "upper classes" as a criterion to judge whether that society is overpopulated or not. Of course the aforesaid arguments did not presuppose any serious obstacle, either political or economical, to exist which would prevent people from changing freely their occupation or abode. In actual society the case is somewhat different due to various social frictions, and this phenomenon will be sometimes slow to appear, or may even be overshadowed by other factors. What I said is therefore a certain abstraction of the general tendency which things are apt to take in the given society.

III

The pressure of population is felt very keenly when there is overpopulation, but it is not limited to this case alone. In a progressive society or nation the standard of living of its people must be going up at a certain rate. Of course our social development cannot be measured merely by the standard of living, but there is no doubt that this is one of the most important criteria of a civilized society. Unless you are the strictest kind of stoic, you will not look upon an increase of material well being as detrimental to the development of man's spiritual nature. A standard of living refers not only to our material, but also to our spiritual, development, as, for example, in its bearing upon the increased cost of education. The desire of every nation to raise its standard of living is therefore a reasonable aspiration. Nations have a certain expectation of improvement in the future in that respect because of the course the standard of living has taken in the past, and if, in spite of their utmost efforts, this expectation is not realized, they will quite naturally become dissatisfied. In other words, even when the standard of living is not actually going down but is merely being retarded suddenly in its upward tendency for reasons supposed to be due to the increase of population, then the people will be dissatisfied and will begin to feel the pressure of population. And, of course, if the average standard of living of the masses is obviously lowered, then the pressure of population becomes even greater.

IV

You will notice that I have taken the general average standard of living of the common people as a means of measuring overpopulation because the standard of living of a small number of millionaires has nothing to do with the idea of overpopulation in any society. Let us think for a moment of the factors which determine this general "average standard of living of the masses." In my judgment they are as follows: first, the productive power of the society; second, the coefficient of the division of wealth between the general masses and a small number of wealthy people in that society; and third, the number of the common people. Therefore, if there be change in any of these factors, the standard of living of the masses will be changed. As a logical result of this reasoning, we know that the solution of the problem of overpopulation must be accomplished in the following three ways: first, through increase of production by the development of technique or by the elimination of waste in an enterprise; second, through changing the coefficient of the division of wealth among different social classes; and third, through regulation of the number of people. It depends entirely upon the special conditions in a given society as to how much importance we shall attach to each one of these means.

V

I have mentioned in part the overpopulation and the pressure of population in one isolated society, but here must be added a complementary argument if we think of the coexistence of many societies or nations.

Suppose there are two countries, A and B. In country A the natural resources are very abundant, its productive power great, and its population small. Consequently the standard of living of the people is very high and still on the upward grade. On the other hand, in country B the capacity for producing wealth is very low and the population large. Here the standard of living will naturally be low, as well as very slow to move upward. Then the difference in the standards of living of these two countries will not be affected even though the technique of production or the coefficient of division of wealth may be the same in both. In such a case there would be no problem if these two countries lived quite apart without intercourse or close relation between them, as America and Japan did before the Meiji Restoration. But once a close relationship is established between these two nations, the people of the one country cannot but compare their conditions with those of the other. They will see that they do not receive the same amount of income for an equal amount of work and will naturally begin to think that their country is overpopulated in comparison with the other. In such circumstances, the people of country B would naturally like to migrate to country A with the hope of sharing the better economic conditions in that country, and many would do so were it not for artificial barriers. Now you can imagine a certain number of people in country B who would not have remained in their homeland had they been free to follow their inclinations. Such people are kept in country B because of artificial devices and against their own will. Is it not permissible, then, to say that these people represent overpopulation in country B, at least in a comparative or international sense? In such circumstances I would like to describe such a group of people as an overpopulation in a secondary sense, which means the existence of a group of people who are potentially migratory. This kind of overpopulation which I have described as "secondary" or "potential" may be true of a country where overpopulation in the primary or actual sense does not exist. When secondary overpopulation is supplemented by the existence of overpopulation in the primary sense, then pressure of migration will become much greater.

VI

Let me now call your attention to the fact that a difference between the standards of living of countries A and B must be due mainly to a difference in the real wages or in the earnings of business if it is to operate as the motive power of migration of the population from one to the other. If there is much difference in the fortunes of the peoples of these two respective countries, and the people of country A enjoy a much higher standard of living because of greater income due to their fortunes, then such standard of living cannot be enjoyed by any newcomers who are not as rich as they. Naturally, the higher standard of living of country A will not then become attractive to so many people of country B. Again, in another case, let us suppose there is much difference in the standard of living between these two countries not because of the difference of personal properties or of wages but because of the difference in the amounts of public utilities. Then the country A will be attractive to the people of country B provided that newcomers are allowed to share in the general benefits of those public utilities. Anyhow, neither wages nor earning powers, but real material as well as spiritual comfort, accounts much for people's migration. Just as the difference in atmospheric pressure will cause air to move, so the difference in the standard of living will cause people to migrate. Within the boundaries of one country it may take the form of rural exodus, that is to say, the city drift of the rural population and between countries it will take the form of migration from one to the other.

VII

In considering the latter phenomenon we should not forget that there are some factors which retard or facilitate this international migration. Among those that retard, I would mention geographical separation, difference of customs and social institutions, and difference in natural environments. These retarding factors may be called "non-artificial obstacles," because they are not set up intentionally with the purpose of making obstacles. Side by side, there are other obstacles which are quite artificial, such as regulations controlling emigration and immigration, and the social attitude created in a country by the arrival of immigrants from another country. Among the factors that facilitate migration, mention may be made of special encouragement given to migrants sometimes by the sending and sometimes by the receiving country. When the artificial and non-artificial obstacles are powerful enough and encouragement or facility given too insignificant, the potential tendency to migrate may not be realized. Then that power may be transformed into resentment toward foreign countries or toward internal politics, and gradually there arises the demand for social reconstruction or international readjustment.

VIII

Now we come to the problem of a clash of interests between two peoples living in different parts of the world, both of whom desire to raise their standards of living and are opposed to having their standard of living lowered. They cannot be blamed for this attitude; yet how shall we settle the differences between these two antagonistic interests? Are national legislative measures alone sufficient to settle the question? To a certain degree such legislative measures may be efficacious, but they do not represent an entirely satisfactory solution. This is because, as long as the public sentiment of other countries is involved, such measures, bearing upon the welfare of other peoples and adopted without a clear understanding of them, are likely to cause international resentment and friction, and thus disturb the peaceful evolution of the world. Therefore, to regulate migration satisfactorily, some sort of international agreement must be worked out. Especially will this become more necessary and urgent when the countries of immigration as well as emigration take such protective or regulating measures as are mentioned by Professor Varlez in the report of the League of Nations. With much expectation we look to the development of political thought among various nations in this respect. It is a question whether sane reason will get the upper hand of blind passions in determining the course of humanity. Fair-minded people in each country can contribute, no doubt, very much to the solution of this knotty problem. Until now, we have depended too much upon diplomats and dreamy idealists; but is it not time for men of science, men of business, and workers who stand upon solid facts of actual life to share in accomplishing this great and honorable task?

IX

To return to our former thought, when the potential propensity to migrate is checked by artificial regulations, conditions conducive to the peaceful

raising of the standard of living must be produced.
To effect this result is, of course, the affair of the
particular nation concerned, which very often, however, may find difficulty in accomplishing the task
by itself, as nowadays the affairs of nations are so
closely interwoven. Here are many opportunities
for international co-operation in attaining the desired aim. To show good will and a desire to help
another nation in accomplishing this difficult task
will deepen the sense of international solidarity. In
the long run it will benefit the country which has
extended a helping-hand toward another. To quote
a Japanese proverb, "Sympathy, like an echo, will
come back to the giver." My only fear is that the
national selfishness of the people will obscure this
golden principle, and the stern capitalistic competition among nations sometimes drive international
politics into bankruptcy.

X

In the foregoing I mentioned that the difference
in the standard of living becomes the motive power
for migration as well as the cause of objection to
newcomers in the land to which the people migrate.

But here I would say something more in connection with the standard of living. In many Western
nations when the standard of living attains a cer-

tain height, there occurs a tendency among people to restrict the number of children in order to maintain this standard of living both for themselves and their children. Thus originates the so-called "two-children" or "three-children" system. As a result the birth-rate becomes lower where people live on a high standard of living while it will not decline where the people's standard of living is not so high. Thus when the pressure of population begins to be felt, one of the cures is to think out measures for raising the standard of living. International economic co-operation conducive to this end is suggested again as one of the measures. In this connection, we should not overlook the importance of the work of the International Labor Conference, which aims at the betterment of the working conditions of the workers throughout the world. It may seem rather odd, but it is not without meaning, that the Labour Chapter was inserted in the Versailles Peace Treaty which has so many defects and drawbacks but at least has one merit—one point conducive to the world's peace—and that is nothing but this Labour Chapter itself.

XI

Thus far I have talked about the relations between the standard of living and the quantitative problem of population. Here I must add a few words in connection with the qualitative side of the population problem. Because of the fact that when the standard of living becomes higher the birth-rate tends to become lower, even allowing possible decrease of death-rate, the children of the upper classes will gradually diminish in number while those of the lower classes will continue to increase and thus become a larger proportion of the succeeding generation. This may mean a diminishing influence of the upper class until, if continued, this class becomes virtually negligible. Of course it is a debatable question whether the prevailing social distinction between the upper and lower classes correctly reflects the difference in the intelligence or character of the people. In a capitalistic age social distinctions are usually determined by the magnitude of relative fortunes or incomes, but to have a large fortune or income is not necessarily a mark of an individual's superiority. In the field of politics the system of universal suffrage has abolished already the discrimination between classes in regard to political rights. The reason is that men have come to realize that the lower classes have an equal capacity with the upper classes for fair judgment in political affairs. In like manner, the inferiority of the lower classes cannot be established in regard to things connected with religion, fine arts, or morals. In only one respect at the present day can the lower classes be proved inferior to the upper classes, and that is as regards the amount of income. Because of their economic inferiority, the lower classes have acquired less refinement and less education than the upper classes. But neither education nor refinement can be inherited, since they are not heritable qualities but simply the result of social environment. At the same time, we very often see vice and selfishness among people of the upper classes. Oscar Wilde wrote in his *De Profundis*, "The poorer the people the more charitable they are." Christ himself said, "It is easier for a camel to go through the eye of a needle than for a rich man to enter the Kingdom of Heaven." There has been too much exaggeration about the inferior character of the lower-class people; and, added to that, we must discriminate between heritable and inheritable qualities. We cannot then approve the idea that people of the lower classes are inferior to those of the upper classes in latent possibilities, though in saying this we are not closing our eyes to the obvious fact that there are many incapable persons among the lower classes. But it is a question whether there is a greater proportion of incapable persons among the lower classes than among the upper classes. Suppose it is so. In that case, as these incapable persons are inclined to have a greater number of children, then there may be some ground for apprehending national degeneration. There are some English thinkers who are afraid that the Englishmen's type is approaching that of the criminally inclined! We should think over these things in all seriousness. We must be careful to avoid too sweeping generalizations and must not take too hasty measures. The soundest method for us to follow is to adopt some measure for restricting the families of defective or abnormal persons without discrimination as to class. Unfortunately, the science of eugenics is not as yet developed sufficiently to be our unerring guide in these matters. If we are apprehensive of a greater percentage of defective persons among our lower classes, then one measure we can adopt at once is to raise the standard of living of these people, because then the number of children will tend to be restricted. Another thing, by increasing the well-being of this class of people, we shall better be able to discern really defective persons from those that are merely unfortunate.

XII

Today there is not only too high a birth-rate among the lower classes but also its inevitable consequences, a very high death-rate. This means not only much suffering on the part of parents but a heavy economic waste from the standpoint of national economy. By raising the standard of living of the lower classes, much of this suffering and waste will be obviated. This argument makes it clear that a more equitable distribution of wealth is desirable either from the point of view of improving the quality of the race or from the point of view of putting our social economy upon much sounder basis. Our present capitalistic régime is not only producing many unemployed, thus giving rise to the problem of population, but it is conducive to deterioration in the quality of the population. If this statement seems a little too strong, it can at least be maintained that because of too much unbalanced distribution of wealth which it stimulates, the present capitalistic régime has a retarding influence upon movements to improve our human stock.

XIII

From two points of view social reconstruction is necessary if we would solve the population problem. It will be the duty of intelligent nations to extend the application of this principle of social reconstruction to international relationships. From whatever angle we may observe the population problem, the final conclusion to be arrived at will be the urgent necessity for international co-operation in all spheres of our economic, political, and social activities. The day of national selfishness has gone with the passing of the recent World War, though as yet many people do not seem to realize this fact.

XIV

Thus far we have seen that the standard of living is very closely related to the population problem. It therefore becomes a very important task for us to find a satisfactory method for measuring and comparing this standard of living. Comparing only the actual expenses of living would be insufficient because they might not necessarily correspond to the earning powers of different peoples. Those who earn more might be saving more; and in that case, although the actual expenses of living would be the same, there might be a difference in the latent capacity of raising the standard of living among those peoples. On the other hand, the peoples of different nations might be earning the same income but their standard of living might be different because of the difference in the amount saved for the future out of the total income. In such a case the nation which spends less per head of her population now will become able to spend more than the other in the future because the amassed wealth of that nation will increase its income later on. Thus the relation of living expenses and earning power must be taken into account when comparing the standards of living of various nations.

Again, the cost of living represented by money values does not necessarily mean the same amount of purchasing power or material well-being. A dollar in Japan may mean more than a dollar in America, or vice versa. This may even be proved when taking two different districts of one country. To understand this, just compare the respective costs of living in the cities and the villages. When farmers consume their own farm production, they do not estimate the value at the retail prices which city people would pay for these goods; their valuation will be at the selling prices on the farm. On the contrary, for other articles rural people may pay higher prices than city people. We must take into account these details and must make the necessary allowances in the estimated cost of living in order to make the figures correspond more exactly to the actual goods consumed. The fact that people very often forget to make this allowance may be one reason why rural people paint the city life in too rosy colors and are too frequently induced to drift to the city. When comparing the costs of living or earning powers of different nations, some adjustment of the same kind must be made. To work out that result, the first step for us to take will be to find the proper average index number of general commodity prices. When comparing international conditions, the selection of these commodities would be somewhat difficult, since goods consumed by different nations are not always the same and, even if they do consume the same kind of goods, the importance of these in the family budget will not be the same. But I do not think it impossible to discover a means of overcoming these difficulties. For example, the bread of Europeans might be taken instead of the rice of the Japanese. If this kind of an adjustment is made for the average index number of commodity prices in order to make an international comparison, the selected goods, as well as their relative importance, might be somewhat different from those in the prevailing index numbers which have been solely used for home purposes. Therefore, I would like to call this "an index number of general commodities for international comparison." If we obtain these index numbers and then divide the figures representing the earning power as well as the cost of living of the different nations by these index numbers, we shall have a means for comparing the real material comforts. That will be an important contribution in the solving of the problem of population throughout the world. Again, in this point I find the need for international co-operation of scholars and thinking people.

To sum up the points that I wanted to make, first, the idea of overpopulation must be defined with reference to the standard of living, and there can be two definitions of it. Overpopulation in its primary sense may be said to exist when the average standard of living of the masses begins to lower because of the pressure of population; while overpopulation in its secondary sense may exist when there is a sufficient number of people in a certain country who are potentially migratory, who would seek higher standard of living in another country but who cannot go out of their country because of various barriers and obstacles, notwithstanding their earnest desire to do so. Thus the problem of overpopulation must be studied from the national as well as the international point of view.

Second, the higher standard of living, tending to reduce the birth-rate, is conducive in many cases to the solution of the quantitative problem of population. There are three means of raising the standard of living of a people: more production, more equitable distribution of wealth and, finally, some regulation of the population growth. It depends entirely upon the special conditions of the given society as to which one of these three measures ought to be stressed.

Third, in order to solve the quantitative problem of population, the standard of living of the masses must be raised. This not only means decreasing the amount of existing social miseries, but it also means avoiding much waste in the national economy. The problem of population will thus inevitably lead us to the way of social reconstruction.

Fourth, in order to work out a satisfactory means of solving the population problem with our eyes fixed upon the different standards of living prevailing in different countries, some sort of international co-operation is very much desired. National legislative measures alone will not be sufficient, especially when treating the migration question.

Fifth, index numbers of general commodity prices for international comparison are urgently needed, and the co-operation of scholars for that purpose should be encouraged.

II. THE POPULATION PROBLEMS OF THE EAST AND THE WEST

I

"The East is East, the West is West, and never the twain shall meet." This is a famous passage in Kipling's poem, as you know. It is rather unfortunate that this saying seems still to wield an influence upon the ideas of many people in regard to the relations of the East and the West. Certainly, the world has become much narrower since the time Kipling composed the poem, and we see the influx and intermingling of two civilizations as the commonest daily occurrence. In due time we may expect to see something new, something better than either of the old, emerging as the outcome of the synthesis. Unless we pay sufficient regard to this new phase of our civilization, we cannot give proper orientation to our social activities. The problem of population is only one example.

The population problem has a universal aspect common to all countries in that it partly originates from the relationship between human nature and man's natural environment. But it has another phase peculiar to each country because it originates partly as a social question, having its root in special cultures, economic development, social organization, and the international position of the particular nation. The differences between the population problem of the East and that of the West lie mainly in this latter point. In my opinion those differences can be accounted for by the following three facts:

First, the white race controls about eight-ninths of the entire earth's surface, notwithstanding that its total population amounts to only one-third of the whole.

Second, oriental countries are, as yet, predominantly agricultural, having undergone insufficient industrial development; in brief, they are mostly peasant countries, whereas in the West capitalistic forms of enterprise have been highly developed.

Third, there is a great deal of difference in the relative importance of city life and of the family system in the East and the West. To this may be added the difference in social position of women.

I shall go into these points somewhat at length.

II

Needless to say, the population problem is a question of quality as well as quantity, but what is disturbing most people seriously just now is the question of quantity. The population problem is sometimes a question of how to deal with increased population and sometimes a question of how to deal with retarded growth of population, as in France, or an insufficient increase of population to develop natural resources, as in the case of Brazil. But when we consider the merits of holding vast territories, the question to be discussed turns out naturally to be that of increased population.

The problem of increased population is one which is easier for the white race than for other races to solve since the white race occupies the greatest area of the earth's surface. In the first place, there are many countries occupied by the white race where such a question has not occurred because of the vast areas. In the second place, there are countries where, although the question has occurred, it could be solved by sending the surplus to their colonies. And in the third place, although there may be countries without sufficient colonies, still these countries have been able to send their surplus population to other countries or colonies without much difficulty.

Now Eastern nations, already overcrowded, have no colonies to which to send their people. Neither can they send their surplus population to the white man's countries easily because of racial discrimination. Of course, the sending of emigrants may not solve the population problem of the country of emigration. One may cite the example of Ireland, Germany, and Italy to illustrate the argument. In other countries as well the condition may become similar after a lapse of time, when the vacant places are filled. However, we must not forget that the interval of migration will mean less pressure of population in the countries from which migrants go, giving hope to the people and perhaps reducing many cases of unemployment. It is entirely different from the situation where people cannot increase because of being "bottled up." It may be compared with the difference in two lakes whose water-levels are the same but where one has a river flowing in and out, giving a freshness to its waters, while the other has no inflow or outflow and the water becomes stagnant. In other words, migration will not be without significance although it may be nothing but a temporary mitigation of overpopulation.

The question to which we must attach importance is not the final solution of the problem but the question of whether or not our exertion to solve it is giving hope and courage to the nation and is conducive to the healthy development of society. As long as man exists, problems are bound to occur, one after another; and it is, therefore, unthinkable that such a question as the population problem should be solved once and for all.

When the problem of overpopulation disappears, another problem, of decreasing population, will make its appearance. Therefore, the vital question for any society is not how to adjust the mere number of its population but to find out the measures of making its quantitative adjustment conducive to the qualitative improvement of the nation. Of course, if we approach the question from the point of view of international politics, another kind of importance may be given to the size of population. But we shall discuss that point later on. Anyhow, when we consider the problem from the standpoint of developing a certain nation or society, the freedom of migration, or having room to which to migrate, has a social significance which must not be overlooked. Because white people realize this fact, they unconsciously desire to reserve vast territories of land for their children's children; and this, I believe, is not simply because of a selfish desire to dominate the whole world and subjugate other nations.

The foregoing is a very rough sketch of one of the outstanding facts in any comparison of the population problems of the East and the West. There may be some exceptions of course. According to Professor Varlez, even the white people are beginning to experience much difficulty in gaining entrance to other countries. But the restriction is not felt with them as it is with oriental nations, and therefore we can safely say that freedom of migration is one great difference between the East and the West.

III

Another great difference between the population problems of these two parts of the world originates from the difference in the degree of capitalistic development. The quantitative problem of population is mostly a question of balance between the number of people and the quantity of necessities of life. We must be engaged in gainful employment in order to get those necessities. Now, when an agricultural country undergoes an industrial revolution and develops its commerce and industry, its sphere of gainful employment is so widened that society becomes able to support more people. But there is a limit to this power. When capitalistic development reaches a certain stage, the capacity of society to absorb the increased population will begin to decline, for two reasons: first, machines and new motive power will replace man power, as shown in the United States; and second, periodical economic depression will retard the growth of business from time to time resulting in many people being out of employment. These unemployed because of the two cases above mentioned have no opportunity to work, notwithstanding their desire to do so; and because they cannot earn their livelihood, it would appear that they constitute overpopulation. In this sense the quantitative problem of population in a capitalistic country is not simply a question between man and his natural environment, but rather a question between man and his social-economic system.

On the other hand, the population problem which grows out of the relation of man to his social-economic system is not so pronounced in non-capitalistic countries, such as most oriental countries, where peasant farming predominates. The overpopulation in those countries is due to the restricted area of the land which has been occupied from time immemorial, and is not due to the changes in the means of production or to economic cycles; or in other words, if we cite the phraseology of Karl Marx, it is not due to the proportional increase of so-called "fixed capital" in comparison with the "circulating capital," that is, capital intended for payment of wages. Thus, in peasant countries the problem of population must be studied more in the Malthusian sense than in the Marxian sense. The heavy loss of human life by starvation in the interior of countries like China, India, or Russia must be explained only in the Malthusian sense. It is not a product of a certain economic system but rather a result of the loss of balance between natural resources and population.

The foregoing comparisons represent, of course, a certain isolation and exaggeration of characteristics peculiar to the East and the West. We cannot say that a certain characteristic never exists in another part of the world. For example, a peasant country such as Ireland had a population problem rather resembling that of the East. On the other hand, Japan, with its rapid development of capitalistic industries, is beginning to have a population problem in common with the West. Western countries may feel the pressure of the Malthusian limit in the near future, and Oriental countries will be troubled increasingly by the increase of unemployment in the Marxian sense. Again, the Malthusian limitation is not simply an outcome of the relation between nature and man because it presupposes a certain social system and the technique prevailing in it; and Marxian overpopulation may not be said to have no connection with natural resources. But if we stress the characteristic points, the population problem in the East may be said to have originated for the most part from natural conditions, and the population problem in the West from the social-economic system. In other words, the population problem is the problem of having less abundant natural resources in the East and of reconstructing the present social and economic system in the West. In reality both the East and the West have a population problem on these two lines only in different degrees.

IV

Now may be considered how the difference in importance of city life and the family system will influence the population problem in the East and in the West. The development of capitalistic industries and the rapid growth of big cities occurred as a parallel phenomenon in modern times, the one causing the other. Modern capitalistic civilization is nothing more than city civilization. City life has left its stamp upon our social life, especially upon our family system. The development of liberalism and individualism, the family's size becoming smaller, woman's economic independence, and the uplift of women's position in society—all these things have much to do with the development of modern cities. And it is a known fact all over the world that urban population is not so prolific as rural population. Thus the nation where city population predominates will tend to become a nation with a higher standard of living but with a lower rate of increase in the population. The case is different in a country in which the preponderance of urban population is not so pronounced. The rural district is usually the stronghold of conservatism. The large-family system still has its traditional influence in the open country. Even though such families become separated and form many smaller families, the mutual dependence of these smaller families is much stronger than that found among urban families. Inefficient people unable to support themselves might raise a number of children, expecting help from their relatives. As a rule, rural families so earnestly desire their lineal descent to continue unbroken that the advent of children is looked upon almost as a necessity. The sufferings and sacrifices of women in the bearing and rearing of children are not sufficiently taken into account, and therefore it is to be expected that rural people will increase at a greater rate.

Thus, whether a nation is mostly urban or mostly rural plays an important part in the growth of population. In the West, urban civilization is predominant, and the great majority of the inhabitants of these nations are city dwellers. Therefore, excepting such peasant countries as Russia and

Bulgaria, most European countries have undergone a decline in their respective birth-rates after having experienced the sudden expansion of population which always comes in the wake of industrial revolution. Such was the case in the period from 1890 to 1910 for Germany and the period from 1870 to 1890 for England. These two countries during these periods showed the highest rate of population increase. America experienced in the latter part of the nineteenth century a natural increase of her population almost unparalleled in the history of any nation, and it is only in recent years that her birth-rate has shown a remarkable decline. France is the best-known example of retarded population growth. Her politicians fear that the nation's natural increase will become so insignificant as to endanger the country's future.

It is entirely different in oriental countries, whose populations are still predominantly rural. The condition of oriental countries might be compared with that of Western countries—say—half a century ago. The birth-rate is very high, accompanied by an equally high death-rate. But will the natural rate of increase of the population in the East decline as soon as its people swarm to larger cities? Not necessarily, because in most Eastern countries the urban drift of the people will go hand in hand with industrial development. City life will tend to reduce the birth-rate of the population, but its influence will be more than counterbalanced for the time by the growth of population caused by the newly opened fields of industrial activities. As the industrial revolution proceeds, the population increase will be accelerated, even in an ancient country like China, as long as the standards of living will not be raised sufficiently to check it. This tendency will only stop when capitalistic development has reached a certain stage, as I have just pointed out. Japan alone among Eastern nations has arrived at this stage. We may expect that the Japanese population will undergo a significant change in the near future. The size of the family is becoming smaller. Urban population amounts now to more than half of the total population. Independent professions for women are becoming numerous, and social position of women is becoming higher. The birth-rate in Japan is, by far, lower than that of India and other Eastern countries. But about Japan I shall speak more fully in a later lecture.

V

I have tried to explain that, owing to certain basic conditions, the population problem in the East and the West is different. To recapitulate, the

idleness and luxury, and robs it of its vital energy, the result of which can ultimately be nothing but ruin. Furthermore, socialistic ideas will not be limited to the social class in any one nation but are destined to find their application in the relationships between different nations.

VI

In the East circumstances are entirely different. Here the rate of population growth is high and the prospect of its becoming noticeably lower in the near future is not promising, while, at the same time, the opportunities for emigration are very limited. Industrialization alone is expected to absorb the increased population. To become industrialized, three things are necessary: namely, capital, technique, and organization. In these respects most oriental nations have not developed so far as the nations of the Occident. The only advantage they have is the low wage of workers.

Eastern countries which already feel the pressure of the Malthusian limitation are now given the difficult task of building up modern industries in competition with the advanced industries of Western nations, to whom oftentimes they must go to borrow capital as well as technique. When the process of industrialization is over and the people have become predominantly urban, the population growth will begin to decline even in the East. But then, instead of the Malthusian pressure, the Marxian population problem will make its appearance; and we may anticipate that this latter problem will come even while the Malthusian pressure is still keenly felt. But on looking round, there is no place to which the Eastern people may migrate. If people cannot go out, merchandise must go instead of men. Oriental countries must enlarge their volume of production, their volume of foreign trade. The result will be a flooding of the world-market by Eastern cheap goods to the detriment of Western industries. Then Western nations will be placed in the difficult position of selecting one of two alternatives—men or goods. If they decide to reject both, that means dividing, artificially, the world-economy into two parts, a task that will be rather difficult to achieve. Moreover, it will be harmful to the peaceful progress of the world, because it will deepen the feeling of resentment or of unjust treatment among Eastern nations. I cannot believe in the practicability of such a scheme either economically or politically. But even if a few steps in that direction be taken, then the mutual distrust between nations will increase, and the influence of militarists—who are always in favor of greater population

from the standpoint of national defense—will become more prominent. Consequently, the solution
of the population problem will become more difficult. The advice to practice birth-control will, in
such a case, be simply scorned.

VII

Now we come to the difficult question of the
significance of the relative proportions to be occupied by probable future populations belonging to
different races. The question has been raised in this
Institute,[1] and the sentiment was th.·⁺ the probable
preponderance of the Slavs or of the Mongolians
is to be apprehended. This apprehension would be
entirely legitimate if those two races had represented inferior qualities of human beings in all respects.
But we cannot say anything definite about it, and
especially about latent possibilities, even when we
admit that they are not up to the high standard of
the Teutons in several points at the present moment. When Romans were at the height of their
civilization, the present Teutons were still barbarians. But who would dare to say that our twentieth-
century civilization, which owes very much to the
exertions of the Teutons, is inferior to that of the
ancient Romans. Every nation has its own merits

[1] *Infra.*, pp. 199 ff. This lecture was delivered first at the Institute.

[[181]]

and demerits, has its own latent possibilities, and any judgment of racial superiority may be reversed according to the difference of the view. It may very often mean only a difference of opinions. Therefore, people who represent a certain kind of civilization, a certain kind of ideology, may be expected to express alarm at the uprising of another kind of civilization or ideology; but they should not attempt to indorse their arguments in the name of the whole humanity.

Every nation is apt to think that it alone constitutes the God-chosen people, but it is time to do away with this kind of mythology. We must try to approach this problem of relative proportions of different races from an entirely objective point of view, if we hope to arrive at any conclusion really meaning good for humanity.

It is evident that today we see the most remarkable contrast of two countries, representing different kinds of civilizations. The one is America, in which the Western capitalistic civilization has culminated. The other is Russia, where communistic civilization is gradually developing. These two show not only difference in the prevailing economic system, but also a decided difference in their mental attitude toward life, toward all kinds of human activities. For example, America is spending many millions of dollars for missionary work to spread Christianity over the world, while leaders of the Soviet government are denouncing all sorts of religious belief as a kind of opium intended to make people docile and an easy prey for capitalistic exploitation. And while the one nation is so proud in being the stronghold of Anglo-Saxon superiority, the other is professing most enthusiastically the international unity of working people in a brotherly relationship. While one nation is limiting the size of the family, the other is increasing its population at a rate quite out of comparison with any civilized nation at present. Both of these two countries have plenty of land, plenty of natural resources, and diverse races in their own territories. Which of them will exert greater influence upon the history of humanity? The world has never seen anything more colossal than this contrast. All of us are spectators of this mighty conflict, and we are at the same time destined to play a certain rôle in it.

The question arises whether Russia represents the East or the West. Perhaps Russia is more oriental than any of the Western nations, as Japan is more occidental than any of the Eastern nations. Russia is a peculiar combination of the East and the West, just as Japan is. And although Russia consists mostly of the white race, her population problem is very much different from that prevailing in the West. At the same time it differs from that of the East in that she has vast territories still unopened.

But I have drifted from the main point of my argument. What I wish to impress on you is that the problem of population is not simply a problem of mere statistic but rather a problem of the future aspect of civilization. We can never find any adequate method of treating it unless we dig deep to its root.

In the beginning of this lecture we referred to the civilizations of the East and the West. I think I had better add here, as the third, the possible future civilization of Russia, which will be distinct in its own way. The civilization of the East, as well as the population problem there, will be very much influenced by the outcome of the contact or conflict of American and Russian civilizations. And a peculiar thing is that Japan is situated midway between these two nations, not only in the geographical sense but also in her ways of looking at the world, in her industrial development, and in the temperament of her people.

What will be the share of Japan and perhaps of other Eastern nations in the coming drama to be played by those two conflicting civilizations? What will be the solution of the population problem of the East? As I said before, the East cannot solve its problem by itself today, and neither can the West, because the world has become interwoven to such a degree that we must solve the problem as one world-problem. The East as well as the West must contribute something to the solution, each being fully awakened to its duties and abilities. In the coming civilization we expect to see the merits of American and Russian, or Western and Eastern, civilizations all combined. Russia is eager to acquire the high efficiency of American business enterprises, and so is Japan. I wonder whether the American public is fully aware of this fact, that the world is treading in such a direction as to open a new page in the history of mankind. The clash of two antagonistic civilizations must be smoothed down to bring satisfactory result to both parties concerned and the whole world.

What is needed in the world now, it seems to me, is a reasonable amount of social reconstruction, and international co-operation in the fields of economics as well as politics. It will bring about stupendous changes in all spheres of activity of the individual as well as of the nation. Only by taking such a step, may a reasonable solution of the population problem or of any important social question be expected. Mutual conciliation must come, and a new kind of industrial democracy based upon good will and sound reasoning. In the atmosphere of peace and justice man will be able to take sufficient precaution lest mere increase in numbers retard the real development of human civilization. Humanity is now presented with an immense task. Such measures as anti-war treaties and disarmament movements are making our future prospects brighter, but they are not yet sufficient. After all, economic facts lie at the root of all important social questions, and without discovering that root, we cannot change very much the superstructure upon it. And all important economic facts culminate today in the problem of population. The East differs certainly from the West in many points, but without the harmonious co-operation of both no problem of importance will be solved. I plead for that co-operation which means the intermingling of the two problems into one world-problem.

III. CAN JAPAN SOLVE HER POPULATION PROBLEM?

What are the characteristics of the population problem of Japan? In a sense it combines the population problems of both East and West. Present-day Japan is said to be a peculiar mixture of Western and Eastern civilizations. Western people coming to Japan are confronted with many office buildings in American style just in front of the Tokyo station and are rather disappointed that Japan—the artistic Japan of the color print and the tea ceremony—should have been so modernized. If Schiller could visit Japan today, he would certainly give voice to a plaint similar to that in his poem—

> Er ist dahin, der süsse Glaube
> An Wesen die mein Traum gebar,
> Der rauchen Wirklichkeit zum Raube,
> Was einst so schön, so göttlich war.

("It is gone the sweet belief, the thing born of my dream. As the prey of rude reality, the beautiful, the divine, has vanished!") Japan, it seems, has not been allowed to remain forever a country of poetry alone. She, too, wanted her place in the sun. The hand which guided Japan to her present position was none other than that of Western nations, especially that of America through Commodore Perry, who knocked at the door of Japan for international commerce. Western influence can be observed everywhere in Japan, but side by side with this the old traditions can be seen operating in the life of modern Japan. They run as cross-currents through the stream of Japanese life. Old Japan still exists in the field of politics, in the thought life of the people, and in the fine arts. Just as America is the melting-pot of many nations and races, so is Japan the melting-pot of different traditions and cultures. This characteristic of Japanese civilization is also vividly reflected in her population problem.

Japan proper is the only modern, industrialized country in the East. Capitalistic enterprises have made rapid progress in the last half-century. The industrial capital of Japan at the present moment may be measured and classified as in Chart I. Of this capital, that employed in manufacture, industry, and mining is confined mainly to large-scale capitalistic enterprises. A fair proportion of commercial capital also belongs to large businesses. In the transportation business a major portion of the capital is employed in big private corporations, to say nothing of the government railways. And the number of people engaged in various occupa-

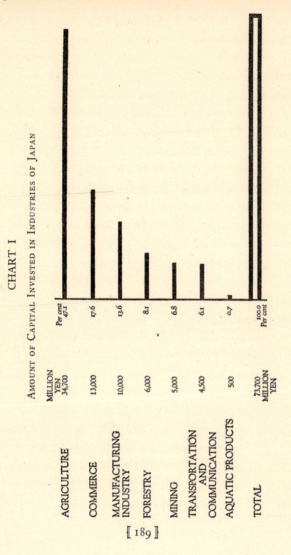

CHART I

AMOUNT OF CAPITAL INVESTED IN INDUSTRIES OF JAPAN

	MILLION YEN	Per cent
AGRICULTURE	34,700	47.1
COMMERCE	13,000	17.6
MANUFACTURING INDUSTRY	10,000	13.6
FORESTRY	6,000	8.1
MINING	5,000	6.8
TRANSPORTATION AND COMMUNICATION	4,500	6.1
AQUATIC PRODUCTS	500	0.7
TOTAL	73,700 MILLION YEN	100.0 Per cent

tions may be classified as in Chart II, according to the recent census.

The total number of working days in foregoing different occupations are estimated as in Chart III, according to my own calculation.

In Chart II it is shown that there are many millions of people engaged in manufacturing industry, representing nearly 20 per cent of the total population. If those engaged in mining and transportation are added to this, the percentage will be increased to 26 per cent. Further, we see that about half of the Japanese population is made up of peasant families engaged in agricultural pursuits. Roughly speaking, the number now engaged in agriculture alone is equal to the total population of Japan sixty years ago. This increased population since the beginning of the Meiji Era—that is, about 30 million—is supported mainly by industry and commerce. The agricultural population has also increased to a certain degree compared with olden times. But Japanese agriculture is anything but a capitalistic enterprise, for almost all who are engaged in farming are operating on a very small scale. This is revealed by the fact that some 70 per cent of the Japanese farmers are cultivating an area of land averaging less than $2\frac{1}{2}$ acres. These farmers are now producing staple products as well

CHART II

Number of Men and Women Engaged in Industries of Japan

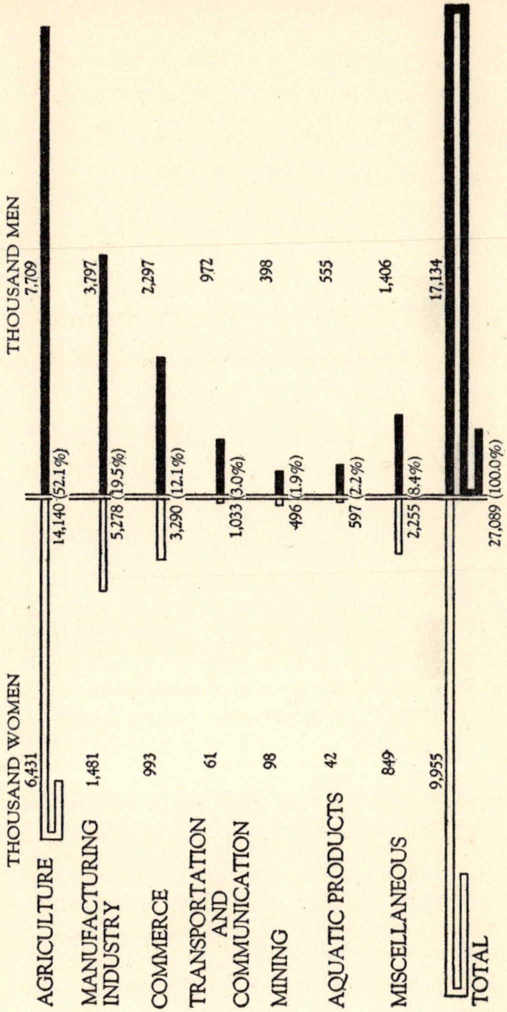

THOUSAND WOMEN · THOUSAND MEN

	Women	Men	Total
AGRICULTURE	6,431	7,709	14,140 (52.1%)
MANUFACTURING INDUSTRY	1,481	3,797	5,278 (19.5%)
COMMERCE	993	2,297	3,290 (12.1%)
TRANSPORTATION AND COMMUNICATION	61	972	1,033 (3.0%)
MINING	98	398	496 (1.9%)
AQUATIC PRODUCTS	42	555	597 (2.2%)
MISCELLANEOUS	849	1,406	2,255 (8.4%)
TOTAL	9,955	17,134	27,089 (100.0%)

POPULATION

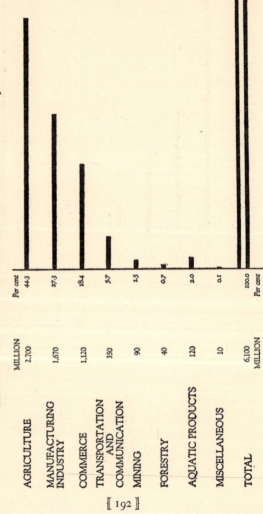

CHART III

TOTAL NUMBER OF WORKING DAYS EMPLOYED IN INDUSTRIES OF JAPAN

	MILLION	Per cent
AGRICULTURE	2,700	44.3
MANUFACTURING INDUSTRY	1,670	27.3
COMMERCE	1,120	18.4
TRANSPORTATION AND COMMUNICATION	350	5.7
MINING	90	1.5
FORESTRY	40	0.7
AQUATIC PRODUCTS	120	2.0
MISCELLANEOUS	10	0.1
TOTAL	6,100 MILLION	100.0 Per cent

as those meant for their own home consumption. They are very industrious and live extremely simple lives. The importance of Japanese agriculture in her national economy is shown by Chart IV. It compares the amount of net wealth produced by agriculture to that of manufacturing industry.

As mentioned previously, Japan is the only country in the East whose industrial development may be ranked with that of Western nations. At the same time she bears so close a resemblance to other Eastern nations that she still retains, in many respects, the characteristics of a peasant country. Without an understanding of this phase of Japanese national economy the population problem of Japan cannot be fully comprehended. Now let us examine the population growth of Japan.

The Japanese population has doubled since the beginning of the Meiji Era, and its annual increase in very recent years is around 900,000, the ratio of increase being about 14 per 1,000. The number of births and deaths and the natural increase due to the differences in these figures are illustrated in Charts V and VI.

The foregoing charts show an increasing gap between the actual number of births and deaths. They also indicate that the birth-rate has increased and the death-rate decreased greatly compared

CHART IV

Wealth of Agriculture Compared to That of Manufacturing Industry in Japan

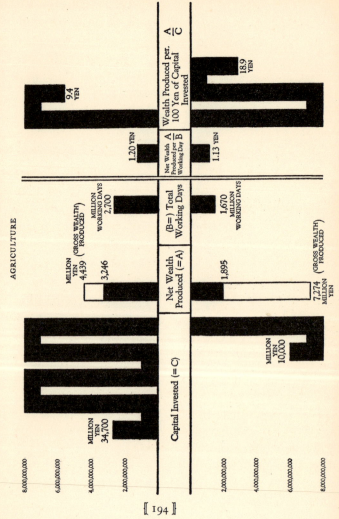

AGRICULTURE

MANUFACTURING INDUSTRY

$\dfrac{A}{C}$	Wealth Produced per 100 Yen of Capital Invested

9.4 YEN

18.9 YEN

Net Wealth Produced per Working Day $\dfrac{A}{B}$

1.20 YEN

1.13 YEN

(B=) Total Working Days

MILLION WORKING DAYS 2,700

1,670 MILLION WORKING DAYS

MILLION YEN 4,439 (GROSS WEALTH PRODUCED)

3,246

Net Wealth Produced (= A)

1,895

7,274 MILLION YEN (GROSS WEALTH PRODUCED)

Capital Invested (= C)

MILLION YEN 34,700

MILLION YEN 10,000

8,000,000,000
6,000,000,000
4,000,000,000
2,000,000,000

2,000,000,000
4,000,000,000
6,000,000,000
8,000,000,000

with the figures obtaining fifty years ago. But the increase in the birth-rate has been quite insignificant during the past twenty years, and may even be said to be slightly on the downward grade since 1920. The death-rate has also declined since that date; but as it declined at a greater rate than the birth-rate decreased, the rate of natural increase of population is still ascending. And yet, if one takes the average rate of natural increase during the seven years following 1920, one will see that it shows no indication of ascendency compared with the seven years' average prior to 1917 (1918 and 1919 were omitted because of the exceptionally high mortality due to Spanish Influenza).

Now let us inquire into the reason why Japan has increased its birth-rate since the beginning of the Meiji Era. This may be due partly to the legal prohibition of measures taken to limit the number of children in the feudal age, and partly to the new mode of living, the better food, clothing, and housing accommodations which may have enhanced the procreative capacity. But the main reason lies, perhaps, in the agricultural as well as industrial development of modern Japan, which made it possible for her to maintain an increased number of people at a higher standard of living. This may be illustrated by the following facts. The total arable land

POPULATION

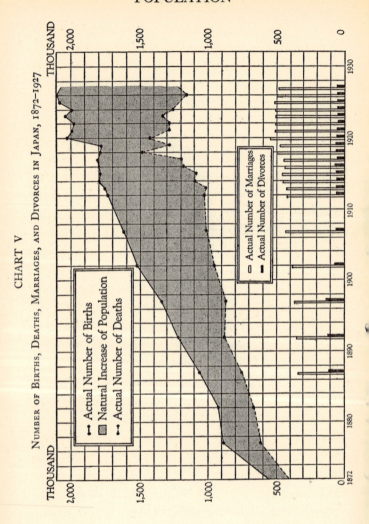

CHART V

NUMBER OF BIRTHS, DEATHS, MARRIAGES, AND DIVORCES IN JAPAN, 1872–1927

- Actual Number of Births
- Natural Increase of Population
- Actual Number of Deaths

- Actual Number of Marriages
- Actual Number of Divorces

area of Japan increased from 4,470,000 hectares to 6,100,000 hectares during the period of 1880–1925, showing a gain of about 36 per cent; and the yield of the rice crop, the most important staple, was just doubled in the same period partly by the increased crop area and partly by the increased production per unit area. Again, Japan, which had practically no modern factory half a century ago, is now equipped with some 50,000 factories employing nearly 2,000,000 workers.

If such a tendency could continue forever, there would have been no population problem of Japan except that of improving the quality of the stock itself. But it seems that it could not be so. The expansion of arable land area has practically stopped in Japan proper since 1921. And as to the manufacturing industries, although they still show gradual development, it is not at all up to the expectation fostered by the remarkable record in the past. Indeed, there are many Japanese economists who say that the end of the World War was the turning point in the history of Japan's industrial development. And it may not be mere coincidence that her birth, death, and natural-increase rates, seem also to have reached or be near reaching their limit at the same time. The raised standard of living and the changing mental attitude toward life may also

CHART VI

BIRTH- AND DEATH-RATES IN JAPAN, 1872–1927

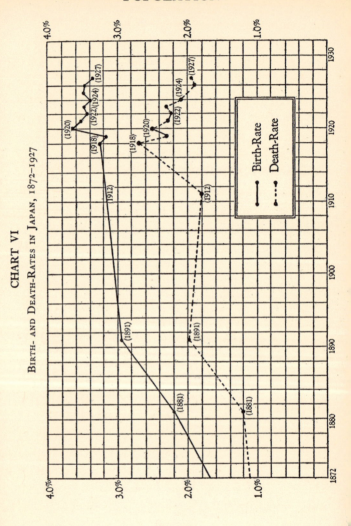

be conducive to these things. There are many reasons for suspecting that nowadays Japan is beginning to follow in the footsteps of Western nations.

Here, let us briefly examine why the end of the
World War marks an epoch in Japan's industrial
development. By that time the main trunk lines of
her railways had been built and the main task of
opening the home market for her manufacturing
industries had been almost finished. The railways
continue to be built, but with diminishing returns
for the capital invested. Then, naturally, industrial-
ists turned their eyes much more to foreign mar-
kets, but even foreign trade could not be developed
with such a speed as before because the cost of production began to rise. This was due to many
causes, but chiefly to the advanced wage scale and
the higher cost of living, which occurred during the
period of unexpected prosperity brought about by
the war. The high cost of living was mainly due
to the high prices of foodstuff and also to the higher
house rent. Here it might be said that the same
thing has happened in other countries as well. But
while the cost of living came down noticeably in
other countries after the war, the downward trend
of it in Japan was not in the same ratio. Under
those conditions the world-wide economic depression, which came as a reaction to the abnormal

prosperity caused by the World War, was destined to disturb Japan much more than other nations. And on the top of all, the great earthquake of 1923 swept away about 7 billion yen of her national wealth at a single stroke. Thus the stage has arrived when Japan is obliged to reconstruct her national economy in all its aspects. The standard of living is still going up, though it is feared it may not be justified by her actual economic situation. There is growing unemployment and increased social unrest to disturb her politicians and scholars.

Now by what means should Japan get out of this dilemma? Her population is increasing, but her national economy does not seem to be keeping pace. The easiest way would seem to be to allow the surplus to migrate to other regions in order to obtain a livelihood, but the practical result of emigration has not proved that she can solve the problem by this method alone.

The number of Japanese residing in foreign countries is now estimated to be around 670,000 in all and it took more than thirty years to arrive at that figure. The most recent figure of oversea emigrants amounts annually to only 18,041 (1927). Of course, it must be taken into account that about 1,000,000 Japanese are residing in the Japanese territories outside of Japan proper, namely in

Korea, Formosa, Sakhalin, and so forth, and also that the number of oversea emigrants would have been much larger if there were no barriers preventing them to go to several parts of the world. Again, Japan may have had little need of sending out her population while she had many things to be developed at home. Yet, after having given due considerations to all those facts, it is impossible to believe that emigration alone will be able to relieve Japan of her population pressure.

Indeed, if emigration could absorb one-tenth of her growing population, this would be a great achievement. Therefore, entire freedom of migration for Japan where there are now some artificial restrictions would not mean overflooding of those territories by Japanese, but would simply mean giving some of them a fair chance to try their abilities. Its psychological effect would undoubtedly be tremendous, because when something is kept away from you intentionally, its value will be very often overestimated, to your deep resentment.

After all, there can be no satisfactory excuse for monopolizing the world's resources by a small number of people, giving no fair chance to others, while the occupants themselves have no urgent necessity or prospect of exploiting them. This attitude is harmful to the peaceful evolution of the world, and therefore its revision is very much desired. Japan, however, cannot expect too much from migration as a means of solving her population question. Here it should be noted that Manchuria and Mongolia, which are very near to Japan, may not be able to absorb many Japanese emigrants because of the low standard of living of the Chinese there. The development of Manchuria by Japanese hands will mean more business and more Chinese there, but not the solution of the population problem of Japan.

The second means of relieving the population pressure is by finding work for people at home by speeding up industrial development. But here Japan is placed in a position with several handicaps because she is short of coal, iron, oil, and other necessary raw materials. Japan has imported 35 million yen of coal, 65 of oil, 136 of iron, 624 of cotton, 101 of wool, and so forth. The total amount of imports for the same year was 2,179 million yen and that of exports 1,992 million yen.

Her most important export goods are raw silk and cotton goods; but these two must be prepared with the keen competition of Chinese goods, where labor is much cheaper than in Japan. At the same time, artificial silk is also threatening the future of raw silk.

Japan must perhaps build up her industries along other lines such as chemical industry; industries manufacturing watches, optical instruments, scientific apparatus, and things of fine art. Those industries require less material, high intelligence, and dexterity, and they sell at high prices.

There is no doubt a big hope in developing those industries in Japan, though nobody can tell how many people might be employed by these enterprises.

At any rate, it may be safely asserted that those industries alone will not be able to absorb more than half of her present population increase.

And it will take much time to build up those industries because workers must be properly educated and trained. Considering the present unrest among industrial workers, perhaps some kind of social economic reconstruction may be necessary to let those enterprises attain their highest efficiency. If workers are discontented and inclined toward strikes and sabotage, one cannot expect to build up any industry with much success. Japanese industrial workers are very much under the influence of so-called "radicals," and they tend to be inclined more socialistically than those in the United States. Therefore, while assuming the probable further industrial growth of Japan, we must admit that it is not an easy task; and it will take some time to accomplish it, notwithstanding the advantage of having a big market (China) in the neighborhood. As a consequence, if the growth of Japanese population is too rapid in relation to building up of industries, some danger may attend the peaceful development of her national life.

Thirdly, agricultural development and the production of more food is an important consideration in solving the population problem. Japan is now importing foodstuff annually to the extent of 274 million yen. And although agricultural scientists are doing their utmost to increase home production, it is safe to say that this increase will not be at all sufficient to meet the need of the rapidly increasing population. We know that the agricultural land of Japan proper may be expanded only by 10 per cent over its present area; and even if we add the possibilities in Korea, Formosa, and Sakhalin the possible maximum of the increase in the arable area may be no more than 20 per cent of the total arable land area of the empire. Japanese farming is now very intensive, but Japan cannot intensify her farming to produce more per unit area without raising the cost of production. Thus, it is certain that agriculture cannot absorb many more people than at present.

To sum up: Migration, industrialization, and agricultural development combined will not be able to relieve the pressure of population if the growth of Japan continues at the present rate. The final outcome of all these conditions would mean, inevitably, either the lowering of the standard of living or a reduction in the increase of her population. And no nation, especially such an ambitious nation as Japan, can be expected to lower its standard of living which is even at present not up to the level of many Western nations. Therefore the way seems to be clear. We cannot agree with the views of some scientists who believe that the growth of population is governed by a certain biological law, just as the growth of an individual tree is confined within a certain space, or as the number of insects is regulated by the restricted area in which they live; because we think the course of a complex thing like human society cannot safely be judged by the results of an experimental bottle of flies. Still, there is no doubt that with certain social and economic conditions and natural environment as a basis, the population growth cannot continue forever. Shortly Japan will be facing this situation if some change is not effected in the given conditions.

Several signs of a new tendency in Japanese population growth are appearing. For example, the marriage age is rising, the proportion of city population is increasing, the size of the family is becoming smaller, and birth control is being discussed in public. There is even a magazine published on the subject. It may interest you to hear that last year the *Tokyo Asahi*, one of the most influential newspapers of the country, asked two speakers to debate the merits of birth control. The question of birth control was also considered by a government commission upon the food and population problem. Here we can discern the changing tide of opinion. Although Japan is fully aware of the dangers of birth control which is so often accompanied by the tendency to make the quality of the race degenerate, as seen in various researches made in the West, she is quite willing to give it proper consideration and perhaps to adopt it on certain conditions.

Thinking people in Japan are endeavoring to solve the population question not only from the standpoint of numbers but also from the standpoint of quality. They want to solve the question in a peaceful, reasonable way; in a way that will bring no dishonor to the ancient traditions of our race, and which will not discourage the people from aspiring to a higher standard of individual and national life. But while reconstructing our social conditions in order to solve the question peacefully, Japan should not be disturbed or provoked, nor should her people be given cause for resentment by unjust treatment. Although the militarists' power has waned and lovers of peace in Japan are becoming increasingly influential, the efforts of peace-loving people may be frustrated if foreign powers take an aggressive attitude toward Japan and thereby justify the policies of our own militarists. Japan's ability to solve peacefully her population problem depends, therefore, not only upon the wisdom of her own people but also upon the wisdom of the outside world.

As I said previously, Japan's population problem has two aspects: it represents a complicated entanglement of Eastern as well as Western questions. Either of these is surely difficult enough, but she is faced with a combination of both, to say nothing of other grave social and political issues. But Japan will not follow the line of least resistance and sacrifice her national vitality and her glorious future on the altar of the immediate material comforts of existence. Inspired by these traditions, it is my belief that Japan will work out a solution of this grave problem, not by using the dull instruments of aggression and force, but rather by employing the more efficacious weapons of an intelligent idealism and the scientific spirit.

THE TREND OF AGRICULTURAL PRO-
DUCTION IN NORTH AMERICA
AND ITS RELATION TO
EUROPE AND ASIA

By Oliver E. Baker

THE TREND OF AGRICULTURAL PRO-
DUCTION IN NORTH AMERICA
AND ITS RELATION TO
EUROPE AND ASIA

The three great centers of the world's population and culture are Eastern and Southern Asia;
Europe, including Western Siberia; and North
America, more particularly the United States and
Canada. In the Asian area, where civilization has
been established for four thousand years, more or
less, nearly 1,000,000,000 people, or about half the
people of the world, are found; in the European
area, where civilization, at least in the southern
portion, is over two thousand years old, 500,000,000
people, or over a fourth of the world's population,
live; while nearly all of the American area has been
reclaimed from the wilderness during the past two
hundred years and it contains at present less than
150,000,000 people. The three areas comprise fully
80 per cent of the people of the world.

Although there is undoubtedly some relationship between age of civilization and number of
people in these areas, it should be noted that most
of the increase of population in each area has oc-

curred probably during the past two hundred years (Chart I). During these two centuries, which have

CHART I

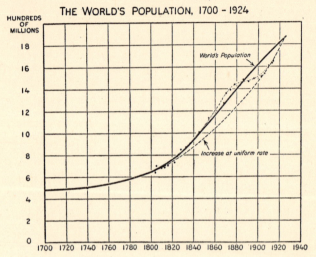

THE WORLD'S POPULATION, 1700 - 1924

The increase in the world's population since 1700 has been nearly three times as great as the total increase during the many previous centuries, but the rate of increase has been decreasing since about 1900. The graph is from G. H. Knibbs, "The Mathematical Theory of Population," in *Report on Australian Census of 1911*, Vol. I, Appendix A, *Bureau of Census and Statistics, Melbourne, 1916.*

been characterized by the development of modern science and by many great inventions, the population of Asia apparently has doubled, but this is doubtless due to peace more than to science, except in Japan; the population of Europe probably has quadrupled; while the population of North America, excluding Mexico, has increased from less than a million, mostly native Indians, to about 130,000,000, mostly of European origin.

TRENDS IN POPULATION

This increase of population during the past two hundred years is the outstanding development in modern history, but almost as significant is the decline in the birth-rate during the past half-century in Western Europe and North America, excluding Mexico. This decline seems likely to result in a stationary population within a century, perhaps much sooner, in these occidental countries, and to augment the present very unequal relation between population and natural resources in the three continents.

In the United States the decline in the birth-rate is rapid and well-nigh universal (Chart II). The number of children in the first grade of the public schools of the United States has been declining, somewhat irregularly, since 1918; the number in the second grade has been declining since 1922; and in the third grade since 1924. It appears that the nation will soon be dependent upon immigration for any increase of population and that a stationary population probably will be reached in

POPULATION

CHART II

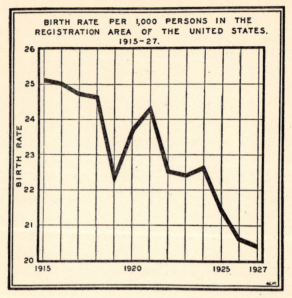

BIRTH RATE PER 1,000 PERSONS IN THE
REGISTRATION AREA OF THE UNITED STATES.
1915-27.

Since 1915, when the registration area first became sufficiently large to constitute a fair sample of the United States, the birth-rate has declined by over five births per 1,000 people, or fully 20 per cent. (It was only 19.7 in 1928.) The decline has been especially rapid, totaling 4.6 per thousand, and almost continuous since 1921. A further decline of 4.6 per 1,000 (to 15.1) would bring the birth-rate below that necessary merely to maintain a population whose average span of life is sixty-six years, which is seven years longer than the average life at present and is probably greater than will ever be attained. The diagram is reproduced by permission from *A Graphic View of Recent Trends in Our Schools*, by Frank M. Phillips, statistician of the United States Bureau of Education.

fifty to seventy-five years, perhaps sooner, when there will be not over 200,000,000 people (Chart III). In Northwestern Europe the birth-rate is declining fully as rapidly; and because there is little immigration, a stationary population may be reached sooner than in North America; but in Southern Europe, although the birth-rate is declining, it is still high, and the stationary state of population is more remote; while in the U.S.S.R. (Russia) population is increasing at the tremendous rate of 2–3 per cent a year apparently—25 to 30 millions gain during the past decade—and there is no evidence of a declining birth-rate.

In this respect the U.S.S.R. resembles the Orient rather than the Occident. If the present rate of increase continues, the U.S.S.R. will have within fifty years a population equal to that of China today. The population of India is increasing at the rate of $\frac{1}{2}$–1 per cent a year; in Japan, where there is only $\frac{1}{4}$ acre of cultivated land per person as compared with 3 acres in the United States, population is increasing nearly 1 per cent a year; and a few local surveys in China suggest that even in that unhappy nation population is still trending upward. In brief, the prospect is that the present ratio between the population of North America, Europe, and Asia of $1:3\frac{1}{2}:7$ is likely to become greater rather than less.

CHART III

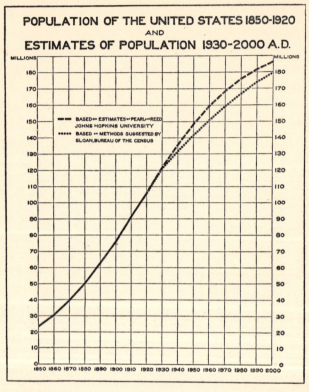

The population of the United States is now increasing about its maximum amount yearly. The statistics indicate that the decreasing rate will soon overbalance the effect of the increasing base number, and the actual increase in population begin to lessen, until a stationary population of about 200,000,000 is reached soon after the year 2000, according to Dr. Pearl. This prediction is confirmed by Professor Whelpton's study based on the trend in birth- and death-rates and present age grouping of the population. More recent birth-rates indicate that the stationary condition is approaching very rapidly, and may be only thirty or forty years away.

Since this condition apparently cannot be avoided, the problem becomes that of how it can be ameliorated—how can the products of America, particularly, be made available to the people of Europe and Asia. This inquiry seems especially pertinent with reference to agricultural products, since the farmers of the United States are now suffering from an uncontrollable surplus, largely the result of progress in science and invention. Whether domestic consumption is likely to absorb this surplus in the near future, or whether it is likely to persist and be available for export to Europe and Asia, is a question that may be of interest to students of population as well as of agriculture, and to students in Europe and Asia as well as to those in North America.

THE PROSPECT FOR A CONTINUING AGRICULTURAL SURPLUS

Whether the present agricultural surplus in the United States, which has resulted in the most prolonged agricultural depression in the nation's history, and has been one of the major political issues during the past eight years, will persist depends, obviously, upon three things: upon the trend of population, upon changes in consumption per capita of agricultural products, and upon the trend of agricultural production.

POPULATION

The trend of population is being discussed by other and far more competent persons at this conference. In passing, it may be helpful to keep Dr. Pearl's or Mr. Whelpton's estimates in mind (they almost coincide) roughly—150,000,000 people in the United States by 1950 and 175,000,000 by 1975, by which time a stationary population will have been nearly attained, according to Mr. Whelpton.[1]

Importance of Changes in Consumption per Capita upon the Agricultural Surplus

Whether a people live largely on plant foodstuffs or on animal products exerts a notable effect on the quantity of agricultural products they consume, directly or indirectly, and on the area required to produce these products, because the transformation of plant feedstuffs into animal products, particularly meat, involves a great loss in food value (Chart IV). It requires about 7 pounds of corn or equivalent feed to produce a pound of dressed pork, and 15–20 pounds of grain to produce a pound of dressed beef. In the United States, where two-fifths of the total food supply, measured in calories, consists of meat, dairy products, and eggs, there are about 3

[1] More recent data presented at the Population Conference indicated that these earlier estimates must be reduced—the number to about 150,000,000 and the time of stationary population to about 1960.

acres of crops per person, of which 2½ are required
for domestic production, and nearly 10 acres of pas-

CHART IV

ACRES OF CROP LAND AND PASTURE USED TO PRODUCE
1,400,000 CALORIES OF THE FOLLOWING FOODS
(THE YEARLY CONSUMPTION OF FOOD PER PERSON AVERAGES 1,400,000 CALORIES)
UNITED STATES, 1922-1924

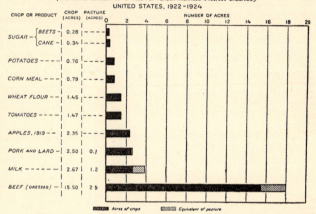

One-third of an acre in sugar crops produces about as many
calories of food as ¾ acre of potatoes or corn, or 1½ acres of wheat or
tomatoes. But, lacking protein and fat, a person could not live on
sugar alone, and the cereal diet would maintain health much longer.
To maintain health permanently, meat, milk, or other foods high in
protein and fat should be added. These require about 2½ acres of
crops to yield the same energy value in pork or milk, or 15 acres
devoted to beef production.

ture and range land; whereas in Germany there is
about 1 acre of crop land and ⅓ acre of pasture; and
in China, where the crop yields average no higher
than in the United States, and where only a little

meat and no milk are consumed, there is scarcely $\frac{2}{3}$ acre of crops per person; and in Japan, where neither meat nor milk are used to a material extent and where the crop yields are higher, there is only $\frac{1}{4}$ acre of crops per capita. If the American people should eat less and less meat in the future per person, it would tend to augment greatly the agricultural surplus; and, contrariwise, if they should eat more and more meat per person, it would tend to diminish the surplus. If the diet of the American people was changed to that in Germany before the war, which was ample, about 40,000,000 acres less crop land would be needed.

This relationship of consumption to production of agricultural commodities is so intimate that it has been found impossible to construct an index of production without taking consumption into account. It seems best, therefore, to consider simultaneously the trends in agricultural production and consumption.

THE TREND OF AGRICULTURAL PRODUCTION AND CONSUMPTION IN THE UNITED STATES

During the past two years the Division of Land Economics in the Bureau of Agricultural Economics, U.S. Department of Agriculture, has been working on an index of agricultural production and consumption since the beginning of the twentieth century. Although the work is not yet complete and the figures here given are only preliminary, it is expected that further checking will not make any significant changes. The index is extended back only to 1900 because of the dearth of statistical data for earlier years, but prices of farm products and quantity of agricultural exports indicate that until the beginning of the century agricultural production was increasing more rapidly than population. In the construction of the index it has been necessary to separate agricultural products into five classes:

1. Plant foodstuffs, i.e., plant foods consumed directly by man, such as wheat flour, sugar, and fruits
2. Crop feedstuffs, i.e., the crops or the portions of the crops consumed by farm animals
3. Pasturage, the other great source of sustenance for farm animals
4. Animal products, principally meat, milk, eggs, and wool
5. Industrial crops, principally cotton, flaxseed, and tobacco

Since crop feedstuffs and pasturage yield animal products, they are omitted in constructing the index of agricultural production, which, therefore, consists of plant foodstuffs, animal products, and industrial crops, the various products being totaled on the basis of the average farm price during the decade 1917–26. This normal farm value of the crops and animal products through a series of years represents more closely than any other common denominator the aggregate amount of labor, capital, and other factors involved in production; in fact, it is the only common denominator that permits combining foodstuffs with fibers.

The principal plant foodstuffs in the United States are wheat and rye flour, corn meal, rice, sugar, potatoes, fruits, vegetables, and vegetable oils. About 70 per cent of the wheat crop is milled into flour for human use and 50 per cent of the rye crop, but only a small percentage of the corn, oats, and barley crops. On the other hand, nearly all the rice, potato, and sugar crops and practically all the fruit and vegetable crops are used for human food. The trends in production and consumption of some of these products differ greatly; consequently it is necessary to consider these products separately.

Wheat.—The production of wheat for human consumption, or of the entire crop for that matter, has remained for fifteen years about 10 per cent higher than at the beginning of the century. Meanwhile the population of the United States has increased until it is now (1929) 60 per cent higher. The discrepancy is explained by a reduction in per capita consumption of wheat flour of about 20 per cent, half of which occurred between 1917 and 1918, and by a decrease in exports of about 20 per cent also (1898–1902 compared with 1923–27). The consumption of wheat flour is now about 175 pounds per person. At first thought this decreasing per capita consumption might suggest increasing pressure of population on the food supply, but the fact is that wheat, which to many peoples of the world is a luxury, is one of the cheapest foods in the United States and has been partly replaced by more expensive foods. However, wheat still constitutes about 25 per cent of the American diet, measured in calories, and is the leading foodstuff on this basis, but not in cost.

Production of wheat has failed to keep pace with population largely because production is still in excess of domestic needs and because most American wheat farmers are in competition with all the world. Consequently, except during the war years, the price has kept low. The price of No. 2 red winter wheat on the Chicago market is now less than

$1.00 a bushel (late June, 1929), which is the lowest price since 1914. The American capacity for production is indicated by the increase in acreage of 66 per cent between 1917 and 1919, when wartime needs caused a rapid rise in price. This increase took place mostly at the expense of corn and pasture acreage (i.e., of meat production) and suggests what is likely to recur when, because of an increased demand at home or abroad, the price of wheat should rise more rapidly than that of other crops.

The present low price of wheat is due partly to the introduction of the tractor and combine, which has reduced the hours of labor required to harvest an acre of wheat in the Great Plains region from seven or eight hours, using a binder and threshing machine, to two or three hours. This is causing the farms in this region to increase greatly in size, and is also causing wheat production to expand into regions that were too arid to utilize profitably under the former more expensive systems of harvesting. The average area in wheat in the Great Plains states increased over 8,000,000 acres in the decade between the war years 1916–18 and the years 1926–28, while a similar decrease in acreage took place in the humid eastern portion of the nation. There are still probably from 25 to 50 million acres of unbroken pasture in our Great Plains states available for wheat production, or an acreage fully half as great as the present wheat acreage in the United States.

Corn.—The decrease in per capita consumption of corn has been even greater than of wheat. Corn bread was eaten in the past mostly by farmers and their families, especially by both white and negro farmers in the South. As the farm population has decreased, and as the income of the negroes and poor whites in the South has increased, less corn has been eaten, until now the per capita consumption is only about 40 per cent as large as it was a quarter-century ago. Less than 50 pounds of corn meal per person are now used for human food in the United States. This constitutes only about 3 per cent of the corn crop.

Corn is the basis of the American swine industry and only to a lesser extent of the beef cattle industry, while corn silage is being increasingly used in feeding dairy cattle and sheep. Corn contributes as much feed for farm animals in the United States as all the other crops combined; and if the corn-borer should greatly reduce the nation's production of corn, it would induce changes of the utmost significance, not only to the farmers but also to all the people of the nation.

The United States exports annually a few million bushels of corn, but the exports have been insignificant compared with production in recent years, except in 1 20–22, inclusive, when the exports averaged over 100,000,000 bushels. Since then, the exports have averaged about 20,000,000 bushels, and no upward or downward trend is evident.

Rye, oats, and barley.—Rye, like corn, does not appeal to the taste of the American, especially the city dweller, as much as wheat. Fully half of the crop is exported to Europe. The per capita consumption of rye has, like that of corn, decreased to about 40 per cent as much as at the beginning of the century. It is now less than 3 pounds per person. The decrease in consumption of barley, owing to the spread of prohibition of alcoholic beverages, has been even greater. The per capita consumption, about 2 pounds per capita, is now only about 10 per cent of the former level. But the use of barley for stock feed has increased rapidly, and total production is greater than ever. Very little oats is used for human food; and although the data are deficient, apparently per capita consumption is decreasing.

Rice.—The use of rice, on the other hand, increased notably from the beginning of the century until the beginning of the World War. During and since the war, per capita consumption has remained about stationary, except that during the last year or two it has been rising. However, rice is of very minor importance in the American diet, only about 6 pounds per capita being consumed in recent years. From a third to a half of the total production in the United States is now exported to the Orient or shipped to Porto Rico and Hawaii.

All cereals.—Totaling all the cereal foodstuffs, it appears that per capita consumption was about 380 pounds at the beginning of the century, but has been only about 240 pounds during the past few years, which is 37 per cent less. This is an amazing change in these foods that are called the "staff of life" and which in most of the world are such. What other foodstuffs have taken their place?

Sugar.—The carbohydrate portion of the cereal foods, which constitutes 75–85 per cent of the digestible nutrients in most of the cereals, has been provided in part by sugar, a pure carbohydrate, and to a less extent by the green vegetables. The production of sugar in the United States has increased threefold since the beginning of the twentieth century, but this increase is wholly of beet sugar, as cane sugar production in Louisiana has declined greatly. However, the production of sugar in the continental United States is only one-sixth of the consumption, over half the sugar consumed coming from Cuba and one-third from Porto Rico, Hawaii, and the Philippines in about equal amounts. The increase in consumption of sugar in the United States has been amazing. One hundred years ago the per capita consumption was about one-tenth as great as at present, and the total consumption about one-hundredth as great. Even during the past quarter-century, per capita consumption has increased from 65 pounds to about 108 pounds, which is over 60 per cent. Nearly two-thirds of this increase occurred between 1918, when the prohibition law went into effect, and 1925. Since 1925, consumption per capita has not increased; possibly the saturation point has been reached.

But it should be noted that this increase of 43 pounds in per capita consumption of sugar since the beginning of the century is much less than a third of the carbohydrates contained in the 140 pounds decrease in consumption of cereal foodstuffs. Has this deficiency been balanced by an increase in consumption of other carbohydrate foods?

Potatoes.—The production of white or Irish potatoes has practically doubled since the beginning of the twentieth century, but production appears to have been abnormally low at that time. Except for this period at the beginning of the century, the production of potatoes has increased only as rapidly as population, i.e., the trend of per capita production, and consumption also, for that matter, has remained approximately constant.

Fruit.—The next most important carbohydrate food is fruit. The production of the fruits, including grapes, has increased about 80 per cent, apparently, since the beginning of the century, or 20 per cent more than the nation's population. But the exports have also increased, and the imports have decreased, except of bananas, so that the per capita consumption is, apparently, only a little larger than thirty years ago. There has been, however, a notable shift from apples toward citrus fruits and grapes. The per capita consumption of all fruit is nearly 200 pounds, or more than of wheat flour, but it should be recalled that the fruits will average 75–85 per cent water and only 10–20 per cent carbohydrates, except bananas, which average 23 per cent, skin excluded. The increase in consumption of fruit is, therefore, the equivalent of only 2 or 3 pounds of wheat flour, measured in calories.

Vegetables.—The only other important carbohydrate-carrying foods are the vegetables. Statistical data on the production of the vegetables are very meager and defective, and about all that can be said with safety is that there has been probably a 25 per cent increase in the per capita consumption of the vegetables in the past decade, as compared with previous years as far back as 1900. The carbohydrates contained in the vegetables are quite inadequate to balance the discrepancy between the decrease in cereal consumption and the increase in sugar consumption.

Vegetable oils.—The production of cottonseed oil has more than doubled since the beginning of the century, while its consumption for food apparently has increased fourfold. The importation of coconut oil and copra, mostly from the Philippines has increased enormously, so that at present the vegetable oils constitute about 4 per cent, in calories, of the food supply of the American people. As they are pure fats, they now contribute a large proportion of the fats in the American diet. Obviously they do not account in the least for the decline in carbohydrates resulting from the decrease in cereal consumption.

Summary for plant foodstuffs.—Plant foodstuffs now constitute about 60 per cent, measured in calories, of the American diet. Half of this 60 per cent, or about 30 per cent of the total diet, consists of the cereal foods. But the cereals constituted about 47 per cent of the total food consumption, measured in calories, at the beginning of the century. Of this deficit of 17 per cent, 4 per cent consists of proteins and fats and 13 per cent consists of carbohydrates.

The small decrease in fats in the cereals is more than balanced by the increase in vegetable oils. But there remains, as a result of the changes in consumption of plant foodstuffs, a decrease in carbohydrates equal to 6 or 7 per cent of the total diet, measured in calories, and a decrease in protein amounting to 3 or 4 per cent of the total diet, while the net increase in vegetable fats amounts to 3 or 4 per cent of the total diet. This leaves a net deficit of 6 or 7 per cent in the diet to be accounted for by an increase in animal products or by an actual decrease in per capita consumption of food.

THE TREND IN PRODUCTION AND CONSUMPTION OF ANIMAL PRODUCTS

The principal animal foodstuffs are beef and veal, pork and lard, mutton and lamb, poultry and eggs, and, most important of all, milk and its products. Animal products also include two fibers, wool and mohair. The dominating importance of the animal products in American agriculture is not generally realized. Although animal foodstuffs contribute only about 40 per cent of the American diet, measured in calories, the farm value of these animal foodstuffs is about two and a half times greater than the value of the plant foodstuffs. With reference to land requirements, the production of animal products, including wool and mohair, requires about 70 per cent of the crop acreage, and an even greater acreage of pasture; whereas the production of plant foodstuffs requires only about 20 per cent of the crop acreage. Industrial crops, principally cotton, occupy the remaining 10 per cent.

Since there is not only a great difference between animal and plant foodstuffs in the amount of land required to produce the same quantity of food, measured in calories, but also great differences between the several animal products in this regard, it seems necessary to note separately the changes in production and consumption of the various animal products.

Beef and veal.—The production of beef and veal, considered jointly, increased very rapidly at the close of the nineteenth century, then remained more or less stationary from 1900 to 1927, but during the past year, 1928, was lower than at any time so far in the twentieth century. In view of the 60 per cent increase in human population since 1900, it would be reasonable to expect a decrease in per capita consumption of beef and veal, but this has not occurred, until recently, for two reasons: (1) a quarter-century ago the United States was exporting large quantities of beef and now it is importing small quantities; and (2) the estimates of production include corrections of the slaughter figures to allow for the change each year in the number of cattle on farms, and during recent years the heavy slaughter has been largely at the expense of the breeding-stock. There are fewer beef cattle on farms today than at any time since 1877, and scarcely more than half as many as in 1894, according to the estimates of the Bureau of Animal Industry.

It seems inevitable, therefore, that there will be a rapid decrease in the per capita consumption of beef during the next few years, and quite clearly the days of surplus beef for export are long since passed.

Mutton and lamb.—The production of mutton and lamb decreased rapidly during the early years of the twentieth century, then increased irregularly until 1912, then decreased irregularly until 1920. Since 1920 there has been a probably unprecedented and continuous increase. In 1920 production was 22 per cent lower than at the beginning of the century, whereas in 1928 it was 36 per cent higher, and was rapidly overtaking the upward trend of population. Foreign trade in mutton and lamb is very small; and since 1914, imports have exceeded exports, except in 1918 and 1925.

Chickens and eggs.—Statistics of production of chickens and eggs are much less satisfactory than for other animal products, but there is the same failure, as with sheep, to keep pace with the increase of population from near the beginning of the century until the war years; but since the war, production has increased more rapidly than population. By 1928 the decline in per capita production during the first two decades of the century had been almost recouped.

Pork and lard—The production of pork and lard in the United States exceeds in pounds that of all other meats, including poultry, and ranks with dairy products, wheat flour, and sugar as one of the four major ingredients of the American diet. The production of pork and lard, like that of beef and veal, increased about as fast as population from the beginning of the century until 1907; but then the curve dropped rapidly until 1909 and remained below the curve of population until 1918. After a slight decline in 1919 and 1920, production rose to unprecedented heights in 1922 and 1923, when the per capita production far exceeded that of any year since 1900, and probably any year in the history of the nation. This peak in production was followed by a decline to 1925 and a rise to 1927. In 1928 the per capita production of pork and lard was practically the same as at the beginning of the century, but consumption per capita was 10 per cent greater. This was made possible by a decrease in exports.

Dairy products.—Measured by money value, dairy products are much the most important class of foods in the American diet; but measured by calories, they still rank second, apparently to wheat products. No change in American agriculture has been more significant than the increased production and consumption of dairy products during and since the World War. Reducing the butter, cheese, condensed milk, ice-cream, and milk used directly for food to a common milk basis, it appears that production was almost constantly falling behind the increase of population from at least as far back as 1897 until 1916. At the beginning of the century the per capita consumption was equivalent, apparently, to about 880 pounds of milk; in the five-year period 1902–6 it averaged about 860 pounds; in 1907–11 about 830 pounds, with a very slight further decline in the period 1912–16.

Then came the change; indeed, the upward trend started in 1915 and was under full swing by 1918. Urged on by the new knowledge of the vitamin content of milk and of milk's other valuable elements, which knowledge was carried to the people by articles in the popular magazines and by milk consumption campaigns promoted by the U.S. Department of Agriculture, state colleges of agriculture, and by milk distributors throughout the nation, consumption rose to an average of 860 pounds per person for the period 1917–21, and then, gaining momentum, mounted to about 990 pounds for the period 1922–26. Consumption at the present time is over 1,000 pounds per person, apparently, which is 12 per cent greater than thirty years ago and 20 per cent greater than in the period 1912–16. These figures of milk consumption during the past 30 years may be too high, but they are fairly comparable with each other.

The shift in diet.—Milk is the only animal product which contains an appreciable amount of carbohydrate, but the sugar in the milk consumed is not sufficient to balance the decrease in the starch consumption involved in the decline in use of cereal foods. In other words, the quantity of carbohydrates in the American diet has declined notably, but the quantity of fat and protein consumed has increased notably since the war. Whether this increase is greater, measured in calories, than the decline in carbohydrates the data are not yet sufficiently complete to show.

This shift in diet from the less expensive cereal foods to the more expensive meats and milk has been encouraged by the large increase in income of the urban population during and since the World War. The recent surplus of agriculture commodities would have been much greater, and the depression of prices of farm products much more severe, had not this shift in diet occurred.

However, the two animal foodstuffs which have increased notably in production, milk and pork, are those which are produced most efficiently with reference to feed consumed by the animals and with reference to crop acreage required (see Chart IV). Partly because of this, the increase in consumption of feed has not been nearly as great as would have occurred if the increase in consumption per capita had taken place in beef and mutton instead.

Before considering more fully the significance of these trends in production and consumption of the foodstuffs, it may be best to note the changes in the third group of products included in the index of agricultural production—the industrial crops, so called.

THE TREND IN PRODUCTION AND CONSUMPTION OF THE INDUSTRIAL CROPS

The most important of these crops is cotton. The production of cotton kept pace with the progress of population, despite the spread of the boll weevil, until the World War years. But in the period 1917–22 per capita production fell 20 per cent below that at the beginning of the century. Since 1922, production has increased more rapidly than population, and the per capita figure is now only 10 per cent lower than a quarter-century ago. The per capita consumption of cotton was increasing during the pre-war years, but during and since the war has remained about stationary. The rapid increase in use of silk and rayon during the past decade has affected the consumption of wool rather than of cotton.

Flaxseed is another industrial crop of great importance. Production declined greatly from 1902 to 1919 and was low in 1921, but between 1921 and 1924 production quadrupled. Since 1924 it has been somewhat lower. Consumption has increased so rapidly that imports exceeded exports in 1909 and every year thereafter, and imports are now about as great as the total production.

Tobacco is included with the industrial crops because it certainly is not a food crop or a feed crop (no animal would eat it), and it is somewhat modified by manufacture. The production of tobacco increased more rapidly than the population of the United States during the first two decades of the century, but since 1920 has remained more or less stationary. Consumption per capita increased during the war years and has continued at the higher level. It is now about 25 per cent higher than at the beginning of the century.

In brief, the consumption of cotton has increased from a third of the production at the beginning of the century to a half of the production today; the consumption of tobacco has increased
from six-tenths to seven-tenths of the production;
while the consumption of flaxseed, which was less
than the production thirty years ago, is now a half
greater than the production. For the flaxseed of
Argentina and Canada, the United States has become the greatest market in the world.

THE TRENDS IN THE MAJOR AGRICULTURAL EXPORTS

Partly as a consequence of the increasing importance of animal products in the diet, partly for
other reasons, the trend of net exports of most
animal products is downward, or of imports is upward, whereas of many plant foodstuffs and of
cotton the trend of exports appears to be stationary or upward. These trends of exports and imports need to be noted for several major products
(Chart V).

The exports of beef have trended downward
since about 1905, but there was a notable expansion during the World War years and for a year
afterward. During the past three years the imports of beef have exceeded the exports, and these
imports are increasing rapidly. The exports of pork

CHART V

SIX MAJOR AGRICULTURAL PRODUCTS
Net Exports or Imports, 1897-1928

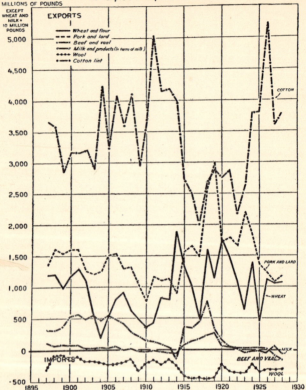

The exports of cotton are now as great as they were twenty to thirty years ago before the devastations of the boll weevil became serious. The exports of wheat also are as great as at the beginning of the century; and the exports of pork and lard, considered jointly, are almost as great. But since 1922 the imports of milk and its products have slightly exceeded the exports, except in one year (1927); and since 1926 the imports of beef have likewise slightly exceeded the exports. Wool has remained constantly on an import basis. But the deficit in production of beef, as well as of milk, is very narrow, and it may develop that the prices of these two commodities will be on an export basis again in a few years. Milk in the graph represents all dairy products converted into milk equivalent.

and lard decreased from 1906 to 1915, then rose during the war years to a peak in 1919, and continued quite high until 1923, since which year the decline in exports of pork has been rapid; but exports of lard have been fairly well maintained. With reference to lamb and mutton, there have been small net imports each year except two since 1914, reaching a peak in 1920. Imports are now declining. Exports of dairy products were declining from at least the beginning of the century until 1908, when the nation shifted to a deficit basis; and, except for large exports of condensed milk to Europe during the war and early post-war years, and again in 1927, the United States has remained a deficit nation since. The only other important animal product from the standpoint of national surplus or deficit is wool, the imports of which have been much higher since 1914 than previously but are not as high now as during the World War years. For the animal products, almost without exception the trend is toward a deficit; and beef, dairy products, and wool have already reached this stage, the latter many years ago.

With the plant products the trend is different. The net exports of wheat, including flour, exceeded 200,000,000 bushels for the first time near the beginning of the century, then declined to less than

100,000,000 bushels in 1904 and also in the years 1909–11, rose again to 200,000,000 and even 300,000,000 bushels during the World War and early post-war years, and have been above 200,000,000 bushels over half of the years since. Owing to the greatly reduced labor cost of seeding and harvesting wheat with tractors and combines in the Great Plains region, a continued expansion of wheat acreage in this region may be expected. The prospect at present is for a well-maintained surplus of wheat for export.

This is true also of cotton, the most important of the agricultural exports. Since 1922 the trend of cotton exports has been upward. The quantity exported during the last five years has averaged considerably greater than at the beginning of the century. Like wheat, the cotton-producing area has expanded onto the semi-arid pasture lands of the Great Plains region, and the use of homemade "sleds" has reduced the cost of picking in this region to only a fraction of the cost of picking by hand. Unfortunately, however, the quality of the cotton is injured, and the lower price sometimes almost balances the reduced labor cost. But there are now two cotton-picking machines whose performance is promising. If they prove successful, the effect on southern agriculture is likely to be revolutionary. Almost certainly, a lowering of costs will increase production, and years when 10,000,000 bales of cotton are exported may become common rather than exceptional.

The third important export crop is tobacco. The exports of tobacco are now about 50 per cent larger than at the beginning of the century, but have remained more or less stationary since the war. Unlike wheat and cotton, there have been no notable improvements in recents years in methods of producing tobacco, and the trend with reference to exports is not clear.

THE TRENDS IN PRODUCTION OF PLANT FOODSTUFFS, ANIMAL PRODUCTS, AND INDUSTRIAL CROPS COMPARED WITH THE TREND OF POPULATION

The history of agricultural production in the United States since the Civil War may be divided into three periods: (1) the period from 1866 to 1906, during which production increased as rapidly as population, and sometimes more rapidly; (2) the period from 1907 to 1921, in which the increase of production was in most years smaller than the increase of population—a period of complaint of the high cost of living; and (3) the period from 1922 to date—years of rapid increase in production and urban prosperity. In order to understand better the causes of these changes in agricultural production, it is desirable to consider the changes in production of the three major classes of products: plant foodstuffs, animal products, and industrial crops, each considered as a whole.

Plant foodstuffs.—The production of plant foodstuffs (wheat, flour, sugar, fruit, etc.), considered as a whole, kept pace with the progress of population until 1906. In 1907 production dropped 10 per cent and remained 10 per cent below the former ratio to population until 1911; but in 1912, and again in 1914 and 1915, bumper crops were raised, and the curve representing plant foodstuffs first touched (in 1912) and then passed above (in 1914) the curve representing population. Following 1915 were four more years of low production, with an upbound in 1920, and an even greater fall in 1921. In this year the ratio of production of plant foodstuffs to population was 12 per cent lower than at the beginning of the century; but in 1922 production rose to a higher point than in 1920, and after declines in 1923 and 1925, reached greater amounts in 1926 and 1928 than ever before. But even in these peak years the ratio of production to population that existed at the beginning of the century had not been regained.

Animal products.—The curve of animal products is much more regular than that of plant foodstuffs or that of industrial crops. The farm animals smooth out the seasonal irregularities in crop production and constitute the great balance wheel in American agriculture. Live stock can be fed for a shorter or a longer time, heavily or lightly, as conditions indicate, and thus absorb feed and give out food like a balance wheel absorbs and later gives out power.

The production of animal products increased almost as rapidly as population until 1907. In 1908 and 1909 a decline in production occurred; and from 1910 until 1920, although production increased about as rapidly as population, the ratio was 10 per cent lower than at the beginning of the century. In 1921 the rapid upward trend of production began, which has continued almost without interruption (there were slight declines in 1924 and 1925). In 1923 the ratio of production of animal products to population which existed at the beginning of the century was again attained after an interval of twenty years; and this ratio was reached again in 1927.

Industrial crops.—The decline in production of industrial crops came later than with plant foodstuffs or animal products, and is attributable largely to the ravages of the boll weevil in the cotton crop. The aggregate production of these industrial crops was well maintained, relative to the increase of population, until 1915, when there occurred a great slump in cotton production. This lower level persisted until 1923. Between 1923 and 1926 the cotton crop increased nearly 80 per cent, and in the latter year the largest crop in the nation's history was harvested. In 1927, however, the crop was only a fifth larger than in 1923, but in 1928 another very large crop was harvested. The production of flaxseed has also been much greater since 1922, so that, despite the stationary production of tobacco, the aggregate production of industrial crops shows a rapid rise in recent years. However, the average production for the five-year period 1922-26, and also for 1927 and 1928, was only about 34 per cent above the average at the beginning of the century, while population increased over 50 per cent.

Total agricultural production.—Adding together these three classes of products, the total agricultural production is obtained. As already noted, this aggregate production kept pace with the growth of population until 1906, then declined for three years while population went on increasing, with the result that production did not overtake the increasing population until 1914. Then followed another three-year period of decline in production, at the end of which production had again fallen over

10 per cent behind the ratio to population that existed at the beginning of the century. Not until 1926 was this loss regained, and only after six years of the most rapid increase of production, probably, since 1890. In 1927 a drop occurred, the first in six years, principally because of a very poor cotton crop; but in 1928 production rose again, and is at present about 5 per cent below the ratio to population that existed thirty years ago.

In 1928 population was 60 per cent greater than at the beginning of the century (average of 1897–1901), production of animal products was 59 per cent greater, of plant foodstuffs 56 per cent greater, and of industrial crops 40 per cent greater. It is remarkable that after the vicissitudes of nearly thirty years, including such a calamity as the boll weevil and the consequences of a great war, these three classes of agricultural products should have changed so little in relative importance; also, that the per capita production of food, which constitutes about 80 per cent of the nation's total agricultural production, should be practically the same as at the beginning of the century, which was also a period of great surplus. This happy condition (or unhappy condition, if you view it from the standpoint of the American farmer) is largely the result of an extraordinary period of progress in production, which began with reference to animal products in 1920 or 1921 and with reference to plant food-stuffs and industrial crops in 1920 or 1922, depending upon whether the very poor crop year 1921 be included or excluded.

The inventions, discoveries, and developments which promoted this rapid progress in production during the past decade are almost certain to continue exerting an influence during the coming decade or longer, consequently, in considering the prospect for a surplus of foods and fibers that can be sent from America to Europe and Asia in the years to come, it is necessary to note what these new factors are and their effects.

THE MEANS OF INCREASING AGRICULTURAL PRODUCTION

Many things may cause an increase in agricultural production; but most of them, if not all, can be classified into six groups:

1. Expansion in the acreage of crop or pasture land
2. Changes in the yield per acre of the individual crops and kinds of pasture
3. Shifts in the source of power, both on farms and in cities, notably from horses and mules to automobiles and tractors
4. Increase in production of meat and milk per unit of feed consumed within each class of live stock

5. Shifts from the less productive to the more productive classes of live stock per unit of feed consumed, notably from beef cattle to dairy cattle and swine

6. Shift from less productive crops to more productive crops per acre, and likewise from less productive to more productive kinds of pasture

The Stationary Agricultural Area and the Almost Stationary Crop Yields per Acre

The principal means by which agricultural production in the United States increased prior to the past decade was by expansion of the crop area. The expansion of agriculture across the Atlantic slope, then over the Appalachian Mountains into the eastern Mississippi Valley, followed by the settlement of California and Oregon and an eastward movement of settlement from the Pacific Coast into the Rocky Mountain region, led largely by miners, and, finally, the occupation of the semi-arid Great Plains region and the Upper Lakes area during the past quarter-century or more, has caused most people to assume that the needs of the increasing population can be met only by expansion of the crop area. The next most important means of increasing production in the past, probably, has been by securing higher yields per acre of the crops and pastures. These two means—the horizontal expansion of crop area and the perpendicular, so to speak, increase in acre yields—are commonly assumed to be the only methods of increasing agricultural production.

But after the World War, expansion of the crop area ceased, the census of 1924 showing a decrease of 13,000,000 acres as compared with 1919. However, the acreage in 1924 was the lowest since the war, the annual estimates of the U.S. Department of Agriculture showing a rising acreage since 1924, with an area in crops in 1928 almost as large as in 1919. Likewise, acre-yields of the crops have increased, in the aggregate, very slightly, if at all, since the World War. The acre-yields of the feed crops (fed to farm animals) decreased slightly; but the larger acre-yields of the food crops (consumed by man) accounts for about one-tenth of the increase in agricultural production, and is the smallest in influence of all the factors. Clearly, other methods of increasing agricultural production are now in operation.

Coming of the Tractor and Automobile and Some of the Agricultural Consequences

One of the peculiar characteristics of the present agricultural situation is the manifold influence of the tractor and automobile (Chart VI).

Between January 1, 1920, and January 1, 1925, the decline in horses and mules, consequent upon the coming of the tractor and automobile, released

CHART VI

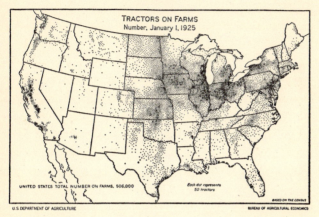

TRACTORS ON FARMS
Number, January 1, 1925

UNITED STATES TOTAL NUMBER ON FARMS, 506,000

Each dot represents
50 tractors

BASED ON THE CENSUS

U.S. DEPARTMENT OF AGRICULTURE   BUREAU OF AGRICULTURAL ECONOMICS

The increase in tractors between 1920 and 1925 occurred mostly in the Corn Belt and in the more fertile portions of the Hay and Dairy Belt, in the Hard Winter Wheat Region, and in California. The increase was notable near the large industrial centers, where wages are high, and less notable on the large farms of the Central West, where, however, larger tractors are used than in the East. Few tractors are used in the South, except in central North Carolina and in Texas.

nearly 10,000,000 acres of crop land for other uses or non-use; and between 1918, when the decline began in the nation as a whole, and today, 1928, the crop land thus released is probably about 20,000,-000 acres (Chart VII). Since all horses and mules required about 80,000,000 acres of crop land for their sustenance in 1919,[1] it appears that roughly one-fourth of this total amount has already been released. Nearly all of these 20,000,000 acres of crop

CHART VII

The greatest decrease in number of work horses and mules between 1920 and 1925 took place in the eastern and central Corn Belt, in the Hay and Dairy Belt, and in California, in brief, where the increase in tractors was greatest. But a notable decrease occurred also in Georgia, South Carolina, and in other southern states, which was associated with the decrease in total crop land harvested (Chart XIII) and can be attributed only partly and indirectly to the tractor and automobile.

[1] See "The Utilization of Our Lands for Crops, Pasture and Forests," *U.S. Department of Agriculture Yearbook*, 1923, p. 456. Later data on feed consumption by horses and mules, calculated by states, reduces the former estimate of 90,000,000 acres to slightly under 80,000,000 acres.

land are now used to feed meat and milk animals or to grow cotton. The portion used to feed meat and milk animals constitutes an addition of 7 or 8 per cent to the land so used in 1919. As population

CHART VIII

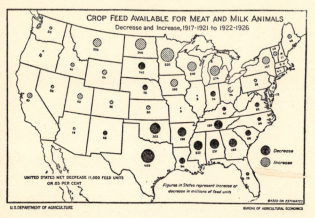

In all the southern states the quantity of home-grown crop feed available for meat and milk animals has declined notably. On the other hand, in the Hay and Dairy Belt and in the far western states, except New Mexico, the crop feed grown for meat and milk animals has increased. In the Corn Belt the feed increased in Ohio and Iowa and decreased in Indiana, Nebraska, and South Dakota, in the last two states because of severe drought in 1924, 1925, and 1926.

increased about 16 per cent during this past decade, it appears that this percentage increase in crop acreage available to produce feed for meat and milk animals is nearly half as great as the percentage increase in population. As agricultural production since 1922 has increased fully 50 per cent more

CHART IX

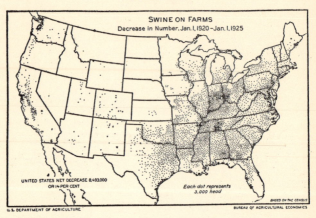

The decrease in hogs between 1920 and 1925 was almost confined to the originally forested part of the United States, like that of corn, but extended a little farther to the north and west; also, a decrease occurred in California. These are feed deficit areas except the eastern Corn Belt. Despite the 14 per cent decrease in the nation's hogs between 1920 and 1925, there was about 14 per cent more pork and lard produced in 1924 than in 1919, and 7 per cent more in 1925 than in 1920.

rapidly than population, and most of this increase has been in animal products, it appears that about one-third of this increase in agricultural production is assignable to the decline in horses and mules resulting from the introduction of the tractor and automobile.

In reality, the increase in feed for meat and milk animals was greater than this percentage figure of

CHART X

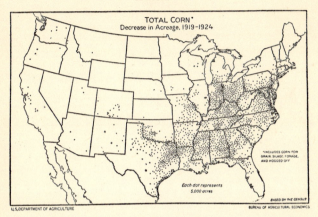

The decrease in corn acreage between 1919 and 1924 was practically confined to the originally forested portion of the United States, where the soils are naturally poorer than in the prairie portion, and was greatest, proportionally, in the southern states. In the Indiana and Ohio portion of the Corn Belt, the decline in corn acreage was only a part of the shift from crops to pasture, resulting in part from the high wages obtainable in the nearby cities.

acreage indicates, for the decrease in horses occurred principally in the Corn Belt and the Hay and Dairying Belt, which are our more fertile regions, where the acre-yields of the crops are the highest and where the production of meat and milk per unit of food consumed is the greatest (Chart VIII). In the Cotton Belt, on the other hand, where the acre-yield of corn is half that in the Corn Belt, and

CHART XI

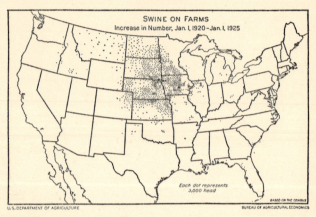

The increase in hogs between 1920 and 1925 was notable in the western Corn Belt and in the Spring Wheat Belt to the north, where the price of corn is the lowest in the United States. In these states there was a rapid shift from wheat toward corn and oats, while the number of horses decreased and the acreage of harvested crops increased (Chart XIV). It will be noted upon comparing this map with Chart XII that the increase in hogs was not quite as widespread as of corn.

where, in general, animals are much less efficient in transforming feed into meat and milk, the quantity of crop feed grown which was available for meat and milk animals had fallen in the period 1922–26 to half that in the period 1917–21, the number of hogs had declined 27 per cent and of cattle 11 per cent (Charts IX and X). By 1929 the decline in

CHART XII

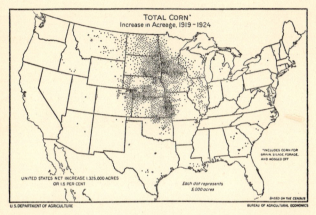

In most of the region where the acreage of corn harvested increased between 1919 and 1924, the acreage of wheat decreased notably; and in the Dakotas there occurred also a considerable decrease in hay acreage. In southwestern Minnesota the increase in corn acreage was in part due to a drought in 1919 and in part to drainage of land between 1919 and 1924. Partly as a consequence of the geographic shift in corn acreage, the production of pork and lard has been greater than ever before.

hogs had become over 40 per cent and of cattle over 20 per cent. Simultaneously, the production of corn and hogs increased in the Western Corn Belt and Spring Wheat Region (Charts XI and XII). On the other hand, the acreage of cotton increased notably in the Cotton Belt, but not sufficiently to prevent several million acres of land, mostly in the eastern portion of the belt, going out of use (Chart XIII).

CHART XIII

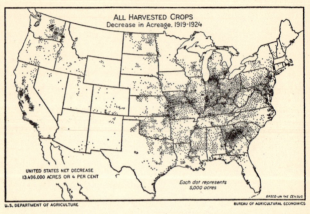

ALL HARVESTED CROPS
Decrease in Acreage. 1919-1924

UNITED STATES NET DECREASE
13,496,000 ACRES OR 4 PER CENT

Each dot represents
5,000 acres

BASED ON THE CENSUS

U.S. DEPARTMENT OF AGRICULTURE   BUREAU OF AGRICULTURAL ECONOMICS

A decrease in acreage of crops occurred between 1919 and 1924 in most of the originally forested portion of the United States, and also in the valleys of California and on the plateaus of eastern Washington. The outstanding decrease was in central Georgia, and in Kentucky, Indiana, and southern Michigan, with a lesser decline in Ohio, Missouri, and southern Illinois. Part of this land was used for pasture and part lay idle. The soils in these areas are neither the worst nor the best in the United States.

Thus the tractor and automobile, by reducing the number of horses and mules in the North and West and releasing feed for other farm animals, have promoted geographic shifts in crop and live-stock production which have resulted for the nation as a whole in increased production per acre and increased production per animal as well as increased production per man.

Moreover, the increasing use of the tractor may cause not only a continuation of this shift in livestock production,[1] but also further expansion of crop production into the semi-arid grazing area of the Great Plains (Chart XIV); and, furthermore, will stimulate probably the production of crops at the expense of pasture in many established farming areas. In other words, continued progress in tractor cultivation seems likely to cause a still further concentration of milk and meat production on the more fertile or more level lands of the North and West and afford little, if any, help to the farmers in hilly or sandy areas or on submarginal lands in general; indeed, is likely to make their situation even more difficult, except those along the semi-arid margin of the Great Plains region. In this Great Plains region, as already noted, the tractor, associated with the combine, is causing a rapid expansion of wheat production into the semi-arid area.

The greater the power per man in agriculture, the drier the land that can be used for crops. Un-

[1] However, the number of cattle is now increasing in some of the eastern and southern states.

doubtedly, a much smaller proportion of the tillable land is actually tilled in China, for instance, than

CHART XIV

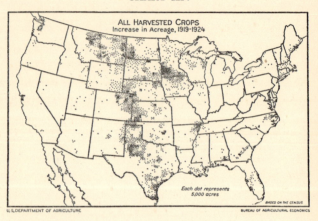

ALL HARVESTED CROPS
Increase in Acreage, 1919-1924

Each dot represents
5,000 acres

BASED ON THE CENSUS

U.S.DEPARTMENT OF AGRICULTURE   BUREAU OF AGRICULTURAL ECONOMICS

The increase in crops harvested between 1919 and 1924 was almost confined to the Great Plains region, which is well adapted to the use of large-scale machinery, and to southern Minnesota, with a few counties showing an increase in the Upper Lakes country, in southern New England, southern Georgia, Florida, and the upper end of the Mississippi Delta. In the Dakotas and Montana the increase indicated is misleading, as 1919 was a year of unprecedented drought and only a part of the crop was harvested.

in the United States. In semi-arid Northern China the average crop area per farm is 4 acres, which is apparently as much as the average man can cultivate with the amount of power (man or beast) and the implements available. If the land yields

and heifers on farms in the United States January 1 in the period 1922–26 than in the period 1917–21, but that about 22 per cent more milk was produced;

CHART XVI

SWINE ON FARMS JAN. 1, COMPARED WITH PORK AND LARD PRODUCED, AND POPULATION, 1900-1929.

The production of pork and lard shows no deviation in trend from the number of hogs on farms from 1900 to 1920, that is, production per head on farms January 1 remained practically constant. Then the two lines began to diverge, and by 1923 production of pork and lard per hog on farms was 16 per cent greater than in 1920, and by 1926 it was 28 per cent greater. The production of pork and lard per person during the past decade averaged more than it did twenty-five years ago.

about 8 per cent fewer cattle, but that nearly 9 per cent more beef and veal was produced. However, after allowance is made for the decline in number of cattle on farms, there is indicated only 9 per cent increase in production of beef and veal per head on farms. Apparently the increase in dairy animals slaughtered, which are inefficient as producers of beef, partly balances the increased efficiency resulting from slaughter of beef animals at an earlier age and improvement in quality. With hogs, however, as with dairy cows, the increase in production per head has been very large. There was about the same average number of hogs on farms January 1 in the period 1922–26 as in the period 1917–21, but the increase in pork and lard under federally inspected slaughter (which is nearly two-thirds of the total slaughter) was 25 per cent. Undoubtedly the inspected slaughter of hogs has constituted a larger proportion of the total slaughter in recent years, so that the increase in total production of pork and lard has been somewhat less—about 20 per cent—according to the estimates of the Bureau of Animal Industry. There were somewhat more sheep on farms and ranges at the end than at the beginning of the period 1922–26; and after allowance is made for this increase of stock, the increase in production of mutton and lamb per head on farms January 1 becomes about 19 per cent.

Increase in production per animal is, of course, greater than increase in production per unit of feed consumed; but, after including the feed released by the decrease in horses and mules, it appears that the production of animal products in relation to feed consumed by the animals increased in the neighborhood of 7 per cent between these two periods five years apart. This does not include the increase caused by shifts from less efficient toward more efficient classes of animals in transforming feed into human food, that is, from beef cattle and sheep toward dairy cattle and hogs.

The increase in animal products per unit of feed consumed has been caused both by improvement in the animals in the principal producing areas and by geographic shifts in the several enterprises.

In the case of dairy cattle most of the increase appears to be assignable to improvements in productiveness of the cows, but for beef cattle and swine much of the increase is due to the decreasing number in the southern states, where the animals are less productive, and a stationary or, in the case of swine, increasing number in the Corn Belt and adjacent areas where the animals are much more productive. In the case of sheep and chickens no notable geographic shifts have occurred, and the increasing production per unit of feed consumed must be assigned very largely to improvement in the quality of the stock and in methods of feeding and care, particularly to the reduction of what might be called "infant mortality." This has been a large factor also in increasing the production of hogs. There is, apparently, about one pig more per litter raised at the present time in the United States than was raised ten years ago.

The increase in production of meat and milk per unit of feed consumed has been a more important factor, apparently, in causing the increase in agricultural production during the past decade than the wider use of the tractor and automobile. It accounts, probably, for over 40 per cent of the increase in agricultural production.

The Possibilities of Further Increase of Production

At present only two of these six groups of factors appear to be exerting a notable influence—the substitution of mechanical for animal power and the increasing efficiency of farm animals in transforming feed into food. Neither of these groups of factors, obviously, can be permanent. The substitution of tractors and automobiles for horses and mules on farms is about 25 per cent complete, and it has required about fifteen years to achieve this result. It appears probable that the substitution will become 50 per cent complete, while it is barely possible the substitution may extend to 75 per cent.

About one-fourth of the farmers in the United States have a farm income of less than $800 a year, including rent of the house and the contribution of the farm to the family living; while probably over one-third have an income of less than $1,200. These farmers live mostly in the hilly regions of the East, on the sandy lands of the Great Lakes states and of the Atlantic Coastal Plain, or on the leached lands of the South. Clearly, such farmers cannot afford a tractor. Their farming is largely self-sufficing, like that of the European peasant, and they produce little surplus. In fact, it is probable that half of the farmers of the nation produce most of the food and other farm products that supply the cities and are exported abroad. It is this half who are likely to use tractors, and possibly a few of the larger "peasant" farmers also. So it seems probable that the increase in supply of agricultural products resulting from the decrease in feed required by horses and mules will slowly come to an end fifteen to twenty-five years hence.

The increase resulting from the greater production of meat and milk per unit of feed consumed by the animals will be limited, obviously, by the point of diminishing returns, not only with reference to the feed but also with reference to labor and other costs. But this point of diminishing returns is not a fixed point, as the classical economists assumed a century ago before modern science had had much effect upon agricultural production. Instead, it recedes with each advance in agricultural technique. Doubtless a century ago, when the average dairy cow gave perhaps 2,000 pounds of milk a year, the point of diminishing returns for the best cows was only 4,000–5,000 pounds; but now, when the average cow gives about 5,000 pounds of milk a year, the point of diminishing returns is about 14,000 pounds of milk for the best cows, according to the records of over 100,000 animals in cow-testing associations. During the past decade the yearly production of milk per cow has increased probably 1,000 pounds, or 25 per cent; whereas the consumption of feed has increased probably only about 15 per cent. Even if this recent extremely rapid rate of progress should continue, there is the possibility of increasing the efficiency of the milk cow in transforming feed into food for many decades ahead.

The increase in production of pork and lard per hog on farms January 1 has been of a similar magnitude to that of the increase in milk per cow, but this gain is probably due mostly to better sanitation and reduction of the losses by death. How long this progress will continue no one can predict, but it does appear likely that during the past decade this factor has been exerting its maximum influence and will soon decline in importance. This same conclusion applies also to the increasing production of mutton and lamb per unit of feed consumed, which is assignable in large part to the increasing slaughter of lambs and the decreasing slaughter of sheep. Young animals gain much more weight on the same amount of feed than older animals.

Both the mechanization of agriculture and the improvements in animal husbandry, which factors have been so influential during the past decade in increasing the agricultural surplus, are likely, therefore, to diminish in importance after a few years. Will other factors probably take their place and maintain the increase of agricultural production at much the present rate?

Of course, no one can answer this question with certainty; but in forecasting the future—and all economic research must forecast the future if it is to be of practical value—it will be helpful to consider the other four groups of factors previously listed.

The increase in production caused by the shifts from less efficient toward more efficient classes of animals in transforming feed into food, particularly from beef cattle toward dairy cattle and hogs, seems likely to persist for some time but to be always a minor factor. Likewise, the shifts from the crops having lower yields per acre, such as wheat and oats, to those having higher yields per acre, such as corn and cotton, may continue for some years; but this factor is unlikely to be as important in the future as it was in the years following the World War, when a rapid contraction of wheat acreage and a rebound of corn acreage occurred. Indeed, it is possible that the spread of the corn borer may induce a contraction of the corn acreage and expansion of the acreage of the small grains and hay crops, which are less productive per acre.

There remain the two groups of factors which in the past have been the dominant factors in increasing agricultural production—the expansion of the crop acreage and the higher crop yields per acre.

With reference to expansion of the crop area, there is fully as much more land, now used for pasture or forest or lying waste, which is physically suitable for crop production as that which is now used for crops and improved pasture—500,000,000 acres more or less. But this potentially arable land, of course, is mostly of lower productivity than that already in crops, or else its use involves unprofitable expense for reclamation or clearing. However, a rise in price of farm products such as occurred during the World War would bring millions of acres of this pasture and forest or cutover land under crop. The increase of the crop area between 1909 and 1919, most of which occurred during the war years, amounted to 45,000,000 acres; and an even greater expansion of the crop area probably would occur again if prices rose to a similar extent, for the tractor is admirably adapted to the task of expanding crop acreage rapidly.

With reference to increasing crop yields per acre, there are almost equally great possibilities. Nearly every farm management survey in the United States has indicated that the average crop-yields were far below the point of diminishing returns. The three major means of increasing crop-yields are (1) by using mineral fertilizers or animal manures, (2) by rotating the crops, preferably with a legume in the rotation, and (3) by reducing the losses caused by insect pests and plant diseases.

The use of mineral fertilizers is gradually extending from the East into the Central West, but as yet has done scarcely more than maintain crop-yields. The use of rotations recently has not advanced much, if any, in the United States considered as a whole, partly because the use of the tractor tends toward larger and fewer fields and crop specialization and partly because the surplus feed resulting from the decline of horses and mules in the northern states has caused a decline of the live-stock industry and feed crops in the South, which has tended, therefore, toward more cotton. The losses by insect pests and plant diseases are prob-ably increasing absolutely, perhaps proportionately. The boll weevil in the Cotton Belt, the corn borer advancing into the Corn Belt, and, latest of all, the Mediterranean fruit fly starting its devastations in Florida—these and the many other insect pests, as well as all the plant diseases, indicate that science is scarcely able with the funds available to hold back the advancing hosts of destruction.

However, the means are at hand to increase crop-yields greatly as soon as the prices of farm prod-ucts justify the cost. The use of mineral fertilizers is only in its infancy in the Mississippi Valley states, and even at present prices for farm products it would pay to use far more fertilizer than is used. The increasing importance of animal products in the nation's agriculture is a harbinger also of rising crop-yields. Although theoretically it is possible to maintain permanently high crop-yields without animal manures, there are few, if any, nations in the world that have done it. Several years ago it was estimated by a colleague in the Department of Agriculture that the average acre-yield of the ten most important crops, which occupy 90 per cent of the crop area of the nation, might be increased by 47 per cent "when economical conditions shall justify the requisite cost of production,"[1] and there seems to be no reason to alter this estimate.

The Limits of Agricultural Production

As previously noted, the area of land in the United States available for crop production is considerably more than twice the present acreage in crops. But, as much of this land not now in crops is poorer land than that now in use, let us assume that production would be doubled only, using present farm practices. Then, if by using mineral fertilizers freely, practicing crop rotations, and maintaining better control of insect pests and plant diseases, the acre yield could be increased nearly 50 per cent, it would appear that agricultural production in the United States, and this is probably true of Canada also, could be increased certainly twofold and possibly threefold. This estimate takes no account of the increasing efficiency of farm animals in transforming feed into food, nor of shifts in the relative importance of the crops and classes of farm animals; but the future influence of these

---

[1] L. C. Gray and Others, "The Utilization of Our Lands for Crops, Pasture and Forests," *U. S. Department of Agriculture Yearbook*, 1923, p. 469.

factors is so difficult to foresee that it is necessary to omit consideration of them.

If the population of the United States and Canada reaches a stationary condition when 30 per cent greater than now, as seems probable, and the present per capita consumption continues, while agricultural production keeps on increasing until it is only 100 per cent greater than now, the agricultural exports would increase over fourfold. Whether this will occur depends on (1) whether the American people will continue to absorb most of the increase in production by raising still higher their per capita consumption of meat and milk, and reducing still further their per capita consumption of the cereals; (2) whether the peoples of Europe and Asia will have more money in the future than they have at present with which to buy American farm products.

Few, if any, more farmers will be needed to produce twice, or even three times, as much farm produce than there are at present. During the past decade agricultural production in the United States has increased over 20 per cent, while farm population has decreased over 10 per cent. Production per person on farms, therefore, has increased about one-third. This increasing production per person seems likely to continue for some years at much the

cent of the world's wheat and flaxseed, 10 per cent of the world's potatoes, 6 per cent of the world's rye, but less than 1 per cent of the world's rice. Totaling the cereals on the basis of tons, it appears that the continental United States alone produces about one-fourth of the world's cereal crops; and when Canada's production is added, the quantity is nearly 30 per cent of the world's total. Taking into consideration the large production of meat, dairy products, vegetables and fruits, as compared with eastern Europe and Asia, it seems likely that nearly a third of the world's agricultural production is to be found in these two North American nations today.

It will be noted in the list of crops just mentioned that the American farmer produces the smallest proportion of the world's rye and rice crops, and it should be recalled that the three major export crops of America are wheat, cotton, and tobacco. Now it happens that most of the 500,000,-000 acres of potentially arable land in the United States is located in those parts of the nation where these five crops are grown. These potentially productive lands are not located in the Corn Belt, which produces principally pork and beef, for in that favored region practically all the land is already in use for crops or pasture in rotation. Nor is there much unused land in the Hay and Dairy Belt to the north. Instead, most of this land is found in the Coastal Plain and Piedmont regions of the South and in the Great Plains region of the West.

Much of the lower coastal plain, especially the western prairie portion, is ideal rice land. The climate is warm and the growing season is long, the rainfall is heavy and water for irrigation is abundant in the many streams, the subsoil is retentive of water, and the land is almost level and well adapted to the use of machinery in seeding and harvesting. Moreover, this belt borders the Gulf of Mexico and from its ports direct water transportation to the Orient is available via the Panama Canal. In this region a large acreage of rice is now grown, but less than 10 per cent of the region is now used for the production of crops and less than 1 per cent for rice. Even in the Coastal Prairie portion, the great rice-growing district, only about 6 per cent of the land is in rice.

North of this Coastal Belt lies the upper Coastal Plain and the Piedmont. This is a region well adapted to cotton, as indicated by the fact that it produces over half of the world's crop. But only about one-fourth of the potentially arable land of the Cotton Belt is at present in crops, and less than one-eighth is in cotton. The few cents higher price for cotton that persisted from 1922 to 1925 promoted an increase in production from 10,000,000 bales in 1923 to nearly 14,000,000 in 1924, 16,000,000 in 1925, and 18,000,000 bales in 1926. Any change in conditions that resulted in a permanent 25 per cent increase in price of cotton or 25 per cent decrease in cost of production would probably cause the cotton acreage to double in size; and so far as available land is concerned, the crop might be trebled or quadrupled.

In the Cotton Belt, and in Kentucky and Virginia that adjoin it on the north, most of the nation's tobacco is raised. There is an ample area available in the tobacco districts to double or treble the production of the crop.

In the Great Plains region, where about 80 per cent of the wheat crop and 70 per cent of the rye crop of North America are produced, similar conditions are found. Only about 25 per cent of the land area in this region is in crops, whereas probably 60 per cent is potentially arable. But the tractor and combine are slowly transforming this vast grassland into grain land. Sixteen million acres were added to the wheat acreage in the region in the last ten years, half in the United States portion, half in the Canadian.

Let us conclude: The American farmer can

double present production if prices of farm products rose greatly or if the labor cost per unit of products and the cost of things the farmers buy declined. Since nearly all inventions and discoveries, nearly all efforts at education, nearly all improvements in economic organization, tend to increase production it seems likely that the great problem facing the farmers of the South and of the Great Plains, and to a less extent of the Corn Belt also, will continue to be how to dispose of the surplus. Since the population of the United States is approaching a stationary condition, there are only two principal means remaining: (1) by inducing the American people to eat more animal products and less vegetable products, and (2) by exporting food and fibers to foreign lands—and exports, in the long run, mean imports of something else to pay for them.

THE WORLD'S FUTURE POPULATION

By ROBERT R. KUCZYNSKI

THE WORLD'S FUTURE POPULATION

The present population of the world numbers about 1,800,000,000. It is very unevenly distributed over the earth. On the average about 34 persons occupy each square mile of the planet. In the United States the rate is about 40; in England it approximates 700; in the Commonwealth of Australia it is only 2. If the whole earth were as densely settled as England, there would be 37,000,000,000 inhabitants, or twenty times the present population. Such a crowding of people all over the world is, of course, out of question. It may, however, seem on first sight as if the earth's population capacity might easily be ten times its present population, but such a conclusion would be entirely wrong. The earth can under no circumstances carry something like 18,000,000,000 people. How much, then, can it actually sustain?

The earth's population capacity is first limited by the potential agricultural resources. The surface of the earth is equal to 33 or 34 billion acres. How much of this is arable? Sir George Knibbs makes an allowance of one-half "for rocky, for mountainous, desert and cold regions, for woods and forests, for

roads and railways, for factory and residence purposes." Professor East believes that 60 per cent
should be deducted for non-tillable soil. The arable
land would, then, amount to 13 or 17 billion acres.
How many acres does it take to support an individual? East believes 2.5 acres to be the minimum for
the earth as a whole, and he bases this belief on the
assumption that in pre-war times Germany "cultivated about 2.0 acres for each man supported by
her own agriculture, France 2.3 acres, Italy 2.4
acres, and Belgium 1.7 acres." But this assumption
is erroneous. Germany, for instance, with a population of 65,000,000 cultivated about 80,000,000
acres. She was certainly not self-supporting. But
the nutritive value of the food she imported both
for men and animals amounted to 10 per cent only
of the total consumption. She therefore really cultivated 1.4 acres only for each person supported by
her own agriculture, and not 2 acres. East, by putting the tillable soil of the earth at 13,000,000,000
acres as a maximum and the average requirements
for each person at, at least, 2.5 acres, reaches the
conclusion that the earth can support not more than
5,000,000,000 inhabitants. If, on the other hand,
one assumes that there are 15,000,000,000 acres of
arable land and that 1.5 acres on an average are
sufficient to support an individual, the maximum

population would not have to be placed at less than 10,000,000,000. In submitting this alternative computation, I do not venture to say that the earth actually might comfortably carry 10,000,000,000 people. The object of my computation is merely to show (1) that East is wrong in assuming "that the world can sustain only 5,000 million) people, unless unforeseen radical discoveries in science bring about revolutionary changes in our economic system"; (2) that every estimate which would put the population capacity of our agricultural resources at considerably more than 10,000,000,000 would be unsound.

It may perhaps be objected that our food researches are not limited to our agricultural resources, that sea-products may be drawn upon in the future on an unexpected scale, that synthetic food production might offer practically unlimited possibilities, etc. All this may be true. But how about our mineral resources and our resources of power? The forecasts of some of the world's best experts in this matter are certainly far from encouraging. Even allowing for all conceivable advances in science and technique, and assuming that all human effort be directed to the maintenance of a maximum number of people, it seems impossible that the earth might sustain more than six times its present population, or about 11,000,000,000 people. And to attain this maximum would involve, as Knibbs rightly puts it, "a perfecting of human knowledge, of human organization, and of human character, which transcends all our ordinary conceptions of real possibilities."

The earth's population capacity is indeed limited not only by our physical and our intellectual resources; it is limited also, and even much more so, by peculiarities of the human character which find their expression in what we may briefly call "national egoisms." The maximum population of say 10 or 11 billions can, of course, only be attained with the freest possible migration. The United States, as all other countries, would have to open her gates to all nations of the world; she would have to accept her due share of the 10 or 11 billions, say 800,000,-000. She would have to forget everything about the national-origins clause; she would have to welcome a hundred million or more foreign immigrants without the slightest discrimination on account of color, race, standard of living, etc. If, on the other hand, the people of the United States and of some other countries which are comparatively underpopulated go on to restrict immigration as they do, it is hard to see how the earth—even allowing for every conceivable advance in science and technique—could possibly double its present population.

But is such a doubling of the world's present population to be expected in the near future? The question is generally answered on the basis of the present rate of increase. The American sociologist Ross believes that the world's population is annually increasing by 1.44 per cent, "a rate which would double mankind in a half-century." The English sociologist Carr-Saunders says that the present rate of increase is about 1.16 per cent, which corresponds to a doubling in sixty years. The Australian statistician Knibbs assumes the yearly rate of increase to be 1 per cent and finds thus a doubling in seventy years. Those three authorities, it seems to me, grossly overestimate the present rate of increase. According to the most recent estimates of the International Statistical Institute, the population of the world increased in the average of 1920–26 by 11,400,000, or five-eighths of 1 per cent, which rate, if it were to persist, would mean a doubling of the world's population in one hundred and ten years.

Big as those differences in the estimates of the present rate of increase may seem, they are nevertheless not of vital importance. A continuous increase of even only five-eighths of 1 per cent a year would mean that the earth which has been inhabited by human beings for hundreds of thousands of years would reach its limits of population capacity in about three hundred years even if human knowledge, human organization, and human character were in the meantime perfected to a degree "which transcends all our ordinary conceptions of real possibilities." And if human character is to remain about what it is the limit would already be approached in about one hundred years.

We thus reach the following conclusion: The world's population cannot for a very long time grow at the same rate as it seems to have grown from 1920 to 1926. If the increase does not slow down, the inhabitants of the overcrowded countries in a near future will have to claim the right of occupation of the less densely settled territories; and if people of those territories resist and try to maintain their immigration restrictions policy, war becomes unavoidable. In case the nations with a relative surplus of territory should win the war, the defeated nations, if their growth is not checked otherwise, are doomed to starve. In case the nations living in densely populated areas should be victorious, they would force the defeated nations to grant them unhampered immigration, and the world's population may continue to increase. But even with the freest possible migration, the limit of the earth's population capacity would be reached within a few centuries.

The terrible danger of a general overpopulation of the earth seems thus inescapable if the population should continue for only a comparatively short time to increase as it has done in the recent past. But must we assume that this will actually occur? Are fertility and mortality actually such that if they continue to be what they are, the population of the earth will double about every one hundred and ten years? You certainly expect that a man who ventures to give a public lecture on the "World's Future Population" will be able to answer such a simple question. And I would, indeed, answer it readily if I knew the age-constitution of the world's population, the number of its births, and the number of its deaths by age. But we statisticians know very little indeed of all that. We do not even approximately know the present population of the earth. I began by telling you that it numbers about 1,800,000,000. But this total is based in part on mere guesses. Has China the 450,000,000 inhabitants which the International Statistical Institute, the International Institute of Agriculture, and the Economic and Financial Section of the League of Nations believe her to have; or is Professor Wilcox right who, after a careful study, assigns her not more than 300,000,000? Has Afghanistan 6,000,000 or has she 12,000,000 inhabitants? Has Peru 3,000,000 or has she 6,000,000? Has Bolivia 2,000,000 or has she 3,500,000? In view of those and many other doubts, how can we even approximately tell what the present population of the world actually is? All we can say is that it is very likely not below 1,700,000,000 and not above 1,950,000,000.

Our ignorance as to the number of births is still more appalling. Many countries, large and small, have no registration system whatsoever, and many countries which have registration have utterly inadequate registration. Take, as an example, South America, where conditions on the whole are much more satisfactory than in Asia or Africa. Bolivia has no birth registration at all. Brazil has practically no birth registration in the northern and central states. Colombia has birth registration throughout the country, but the results are wholly inacceptable, the birth-rate for instance of the state of Magdalena fluctuating from 1915 to 1926 between 7 and 56 per 1,000. Conditions are not much better in Ecuador and Venezuela. The Statistical Office of Paraguay assumes that 30 per cent have to be added to the registered births in order to obtain the actual figures. In Peru the number of registered births has increased from 59,000 in 1923 to 140,000 in 1926 but is still lower than the actual number of births, although the director of public health complains that many births are registered twice. In Argentina no births have been reported since 1917 from the national territories, and registration must be quite inadequate in at least those four provinces where the reported male births exceed the reported female births by over 25 per cent. Birth records seem to have recently become fairly complete in Chile and have apparently been so for many years in Uruguay. The total yearly number of births in South America may be 2,000,000 or 3,000,000 or 4,000,000. For China a guess of 9,000,000 would be quite as justified as a guess of 18,000,000. Professor Ross tells us that daily 150,000 children are born in the world. But why 150,000? Why not 130,000, or rather 200,-000 as Professor East assumes? One hundred and fifty thousand births per day means 55,000,000 births per year. Maybe this figure is right. But our actual knowledge of the facts merely allows us to say that the yearly number of births is very likely not lower than 45,000,000 and not higher than 75,000,000 and that the yearly number of deaths is very likely not lower than 35,000,000 and not higher than 60,000,000.

You will perhaps object that you do not worry

particularly about the actual numbers of births and deaths and that all you are interested in is the excess of births over deaths, which as I told you seems to be about five-eighths of 1 per cent, or 11,400,000 a year. You will be interested in the actual numbers, if at all, only in so far as you would like to see this excess of births over deaths of 11,400,000 brought about by as small a number of births and deaths as possible. You would probably consider it a terrible waste of human energy if it was the result of, say 64,400,000 births and 53,000,000 deaths and would very much prefer to let it be the result of, say, 24,400,000 births and 13,000,000 deaths. But, incredible as it may sound, with 24,400,000 births a year fertility would have reached so low a level that mankind would die out before long no matter how low mortality be reduced.

A very simple computation will show you the truth of this apparently amazing statement. Let us suppose the total present number of women from fifteen to fifty years to be 450,000,000 and let us suppose that they bear each year 24,400,000 children, say 12,400,000 boys and 12,000,000 girls. Let us suppose that none of those girls die before having passed through child-bearing age, that is, before having reached fifty years. We would then in fifty years from now have 12,000,000 females of fifteen years, 12,000,000 of sixteen years, etc., or altogether 420,000,000 from fifteen to fifty years. You will notice that even if none of the girls die, the number of women of child-bearing age will be reduced within fifty years from 450,000,000 to 420,000,000, or in the proportion of 100 to 93. If the fertility rate of the 420,000,000 is then the same as that of the 450,000,000 of fifty years before, they would not bear more than 11,200,000 instead of 12,000,000 girls, and after another fifty years the women of child-bearing age would number only 392,000,000. Those 392,000,000 would bear 10,450,000 girls only, etc. You see that even with no mortality whatsoever, the number of women of child-bearing age would constantly decrease and so would the number of births, if fertility remains the same.

How is it to be explained that in the fictitious case which we have just considered, the population is dying out in spite of the fact that the present excess of births over deaths constitutes five-eighths of 1 per cent of the population? The reason is that fertility was so low that the women of child-bearing age did not reproduce themselves; each 100 gave birth to only 93 future mothers.

We have seen that the world's population apparently increases by about five-eighths of 1 per cent per year. We know that if that rate of increase were to persist, the population would double within one hundred and ten years. But we now also know that the present rate of increase does not at all indicate what will be the future rate of increase if fertility and mortality remain what they actually are. We have indeed seen in a fictitious case that a population with a present rate of increase of five-eighths of 1 per cent may in the future decrease by 7 per cent in each generation, even if fertility and mortality remain what they are.

The question then arises: Has this fictitious case any practical bearing on the problem in which we are interested? My answer is: It has—for the very simple reason that this fictitious case represents the actual conditions in a very important part of the world. The Institute of Economics of the Brookings Institution, in Washington, has recently published a volume on *The Balance of Births and Deaths in Western and Northern Europe*. It covers Great Britain and Ireland, France, Belgium, Holland, Switzerland, Germany, Denmark, Norway, Sweden, and Finland. This area in 1926 had a population of 188,000,000, that is, 10 or 11 per cent of the world's population, and had an excess of births over deaths amounting to five-eighths of 1 per cent, that is, exactly the same rate as we found for the world as a whole. Yet, notwithstanding the fact that there occurred 3,613,000 births as against 2,449,000 deaths, fertility was already so low that the population no longer reproduced itself but had a virtual deficit of about 7 per cent. As the above-mentioned volume states:

> According to the fertility and mortality in Western and Northern Europe in 1926, 100 mothers give birth to 93 future mothers only. With the fertility of 1926 the population is bound to die out unless mortality of potential mothers decreases beyond reasonable expectations. And fertility continued its downward path in 1927.

Why is it then that the population of Western and Northern Europe is still increasing? The reason is easy to understand. In the present population of those countries the proportion of women of child-bearing age is particularly large and the proportion of young children and old persons particularly low. The number of old persons is comparatively low because the generation born in the fifties and sixties of the last century was considerably reduced by a high infant mortality and by emigration. The number of young children is comparatively low because the number of births has considerably declined. It goes without saying that a large proportion of women of child-bearing age tends to swell the number of births and that a small proportion of young children and of old persons tends to lower the number of deaths. But it is also evident that the persons between fifteen and fifty years who now are so numerous will grow older and will thereby swell those age-groups where death claims most victims, while there are not sufficient children to fill up the age-groups which are more or less secure against death and which contribute most to the reproduction of the population. With fertility and mortality as they have prevailed for some time, the rate of increase is bound to decline and to make place before long to an actual decrease.

Are similar conditions to be found in other parts of the world? Does the rate of increase elsewhere convey as untrue a picture of the rate of reproduction as in Western and Northern Europe? The Institute of Economics is now extending its studies on the balance of births and deaths to other parts of the world, and I hesitate to venture an opinion on the results of those studies before they are completed. But a few remarks may not be out of place. Dublin and Lotka, some years ago, found that while the rate of natural increase of the white population of the United States in 1920 was 1.1 per cent, one-half of the increase was due to the age-constitution, which tends to swell the number of births and to lower the number of deaths. In the meantime mortality has decreased, but fertility has decreased much more, so that the genuine rate of increase is certainly lower than it was in 1920. Even without having accurate data at our disposal for all the countries involved, we may then at least say this much, namely, that the populations of Western and Northern Europe, North America, and Australia combined no longer reproduce themselves. These countries, however, were responsible for about one-fourth of the world's population increase from 1920 to 1926. If their population in the future remains stable instead of increasing, and if in all other countries the population increases at the rate which apparently prevailed from 1920 to 1926, mankind will double in one hundred and fifty instead of one hundred and ten years.

But are there not perhaps countries where the age-constitution of the population is such that the present rate of increase lags behind their actual reproduction rate? Such a state of affairs, of course, is perfectly conceivable. Let us assume a nation which for many years has had a stable birth-rate and a stable death-rate, both being rather low; such a nation very likely would have a larger proportion of old people than other nations with a rapidly increasing population. Let us further assume that mass emigration, epidemics, or war had wiped out the majority of the people in the reproductive age-groups. For some time to come, the rate of increase would then necessarily be very slight, since the birth-rate would decrease while the death-rate (on account of the preponderance of old people) might increase. But when the old generation dies, it will not be fully replaced by the now decimated reproductive age-groups, while there will be sufficient children to fill the gaps in the reproductive age-groups. If, then, fertility and mortality remain what they are, the birth-rate will again increase and the death-rate decrease. A nation with an age-constitution which tends to swell the number of deaths and to lower the number of births is therefore quite conceivable. But I do not know of any such nation. There are countries where some of the necessary conditions are fulfilled. Russia, for instance, has an enormous proportion of young children and her reproductive age-groups have been decimated by war and starvation, so that one might assume that her age-constitution tends to swell the number of deaths, but she has so few old people (only as many over forty-five as under five) that her death-rate after all is smaller than corresponds to her true mortality.

We thus reach the following conclusion: If fertility and mortality remain what they are, it will take mankind more, and possibly much more, than one hundred and fifty years to double its numbers. In the meantime, the race composition of the world, and especially of Europe, would have considerably changed, since the Anglo-Saxons, Germans, Scandinavians, and French no longer reproduce themselves, while the Slavs still have an enormous genuine growth. As a consequence thereof, the proportion of Slavs would greatly increase. This by itself would not mean something unheard of. For a long time the Slavic population of Europe has increased much more than the Teutonic, and the Teutonic much more than the Romance. It has indeed been estimated that in the course of the nineteenth century the Romance element decreased from three-eighths to one-fourth, while the Slav element rose from one-fourth to three-eighths and the Teutonic element all the time comprised three-eighths. It would be rather irrelevant if in the future the proportion of Slavs in Europe increased not only at the cost of the Romance but also at the cost of the Teutonic race; it would be rather irrelevant—as long as the Romance and the Teutonic races maintain their own. But once the countries which they inhabit become dependent on immigration in order to keep up population, the Slavs will flock in. They will come because they will find opportunities to work at fair wages and they will be welcome, because—notwithstanding all the eloquently praised blessings of depopulation—no nation wants deserted farms, closed factories, vacant houses, less tax-payers. What would be the outcome of such mass immigration, whether and where the Slavs would be assimilated or, on the contrary, become the dominant race, is impossible to predict just as it is impossible to predict whether the people who would occupy the vacant places in North America and Australia would be white or colored.

We have thus far assumed all the time that fertility and mortality will remain what they are. But fertility and mortality may change as they have changed in former times. How will this affect the future population of the world? In order to answer this question, one should know what fertility and mortality will actually be; and this, of course, no one knows. But it is possible, at least for Western and Northern Europe, America, and Australia, to form some idea of the possibilities involved. Mortality in all likelihood will not increase; it will rather decline. But the future reduction of mortality in those ages which are the only decisive ones for reproduction, namely the ages under fifty years, cannot be very great after all that has already been accomplished. Half a century ago, 30 or 40 per cent of the newly born girls were cut off from motherhood by premature death; today those victims number 15 per cent only. The margin left for improvement is therefore very scant. Even a reduction from 15 to 10 per cent, welcome as it would be, could not essentially affect the trend of population. As to fertility, the range of possibilities is certainly much larger. Fertility might increase again, and there are people who predict that such an increase will occur with increasing prosperity. But an increase of prosperity so far as a rule has not resulted in an increase of fertility. There are, on the other hand, people who predict that fertility will further decrease. A recent article on the birth-control movement thus says:

At the present time it is gathering force throughout the world, and there seems little doubt that the next few decades will see its practically universal acceptance in Europe and America and their dominions, and its considerable advance in the East.[1]

A great deal will depend, indeed, upon whether considerable advance of the birth-control movement in the East will accompany its practically universal acceptance in Europe and North America. If, by any chance, the movement in the East should

[1] C. V. Drysdale, "The Birth Control Movement after a Century's Agitation," *Current History*, June, 1929, p. 386.

be delayed, the Mongolian race might find birth restriction not particularly urgent, because there would be outside of its own countries vacant territories in which to settle down.

As matters stand, there is no real danger of a general overpopulation. Mankind will probably increase much slower than most people nowadays believe. The Anglo-Saxons, the Germans, the Scandinavians, and the French will very likely retrogress in the course of this century; and since the Slavs and some other races will continue to grow, the proportion of the Teutonic and the French race will diminish even more quickly than their absolute numbers. It is hard to see how this process might effectively be stopped. But it will be accelerated if the birth-restriction movement should continue to be most successful among those nations which no longer reproduce themselves.

INDEX

INDEX

INDEX

POPULATION

INDEX

INDEX

⟦ PRINTED IN U·S·A ⟧